PENGUIN WRITERS' GUIDES

Improve Your Spelling

George Davidson is a former senior editor with Chambers
Harrap. In addition to writing dictionaries and thesauruses,
he is the author of several books on English grammar, usage,
spelling and vocabulary. He lives in Edinburgh.

The Penguin Writers' Guides

PENGUIN WRITERS' GUIDES

Improve Your Spelling

GEORGE DAVIDSON

PENGUIN BOOKS

w York 10014, USA
Penguin Group (Canada), 10 Alcorn Avenue, Toronto, Ontario, Canada M4V 3B2
(a division of Pearson Penguin Canada Inc.)
Penguin Ireland, 25 St Stephen's Green, Dublin 2, Ireland
(a division of Penguin Books Ltd)
Penguin Group (Australia), 250 Camberwell Road,
Camberwell, Victoria 3124, Australia (a division of Pearson Australia Group Pty Ltd)
Penguin Books India Pvt Ltd, 11 Community Centre,
Panchsheel Park, New Delhi – 110 017, India
Penguin Group (NZ), cnr Airborne and Rosedale Roads, Albany,
Auckland 1310, New Zealand (a division of Pearson New Zealand Ltd)
Penguin Books (South Africa) (Pty) Ltd, 24 Sturdee Avenue,
Rosebank 2196, South Africa

Penguin Books Ltd, Registered Offices: 80 Strand, London WC2R 0RL, England

www.penguin.com

First published 2005
1

Set in 11/13 pt Adobe Minion
Typeset by Rowland Phototypesetting Ltd, Bury St Edmunds, Suffolk
Printed in England by Clays Ltd, St Ives plc

Contents

Preface

> *. . . my spelling is Wobbly. It's good spelling but it*
> *Wobbles, and the letters get in the wrong places.*
>
> A A Milne, *Winnie-the-Pooh*

If you are looking at this book, it is perhaps because, like Pooh, you know your spelling is a little 'wobbly'. It may be 'good spelling' – good enough at least for your own personal use – but you know that it is not really adequate in contexts where a more *conventional* approach to spelling is expected. Essays, reports, exam papers, formal letters, office memos, minutes of meetings – all these require accurate, correct spelling, and you know that yours 'wobbles'.

English spelling is, unfortunately, full of traps and snares, such as silent letters, double letters and different spellings for the same sound. This book will guide you through them all. It covers the basic broad rules of English spelling (our spelling is not quite as unsystematic and unpredictable as it is sometimes said to be, and the main rules are not difficult to grasp) as well as looking in more detail at the areas of spelling that cause most problems for poor spellers. In addition, some useful techniques are suggested for both checking and improving your spelling.

For many people, however, it is not only the letters used to spell words that cause problems but also the other marks that are so important in spelling – the hyphens, the apostrophes and the accents. These too are fully explained.

When you have worked your way through this book, you will find that your spelling will no longer be wobbly: you will be able to spell with accuracy and confidence.

You may, of course, not want to work through this book systematically from beginning to end. You don't need to. *Improve Your Spelling* is designed to be equally useful for systematic study, for casual browsing and for quick checking of particular points you are uncertain about. By consulting the indexes at the back of the book, you can quickly and easily home in on any point you want to check.

This book assumes no prior knowledge in the reader (apart from a basic knowledge of English). It is therefore suitable for native speakers and learners alike. Technical terms have been kept to a minimum, but they have not been avoided altogether, as they are often useful labels that assist explanations. Technical terms that are likely to be unfamiliar to the general reader are explained at the point where they are first introduced, and all technical terms are fully explained in an appendix at the end of the book.

The variety of English described in this book is British English. American English differs from British English in many respects (in spelling and punctuation as well as in vocabulary and grammar), and the main spelling differences between these two major forms of English are described in Chapter 18.

Symbols used in this book

✗ indicates an incorrect spelling.
✓ draws attention to a correct spelling.

★ indicates a memory aid or mnemonic.
!! indicates a spelling requiring particular care.

Forward slashes // enclose speech sounds. For example, the sound /ay/ as in *pay, tail* or *major,* or the sound /k/ as in *cat, keep, chasm* or *queen.*

Speech sounds

The speech sounds of English are indicated as shown below.

Vowel sounds

Different accents of English have different numbers of vowel sounds and differ in the use or distribution of the vowel sounds that they have. The following is a fairly standard list of the English vowel sounds, but it may include vowel distinctions that are not made in your accent and omit vowel distinctions that feature in your accent. The presence or absence of such vowel sounds in the list below, and in the book as a whole, does not affect the explanations of the spelling rules.

/a/ as in *at, cash, blank,* etc
/ah/ as in *car, palm, aunt,* etc
/air/ as in *air, care, bear,* etc

/aw/ as in *saw, daughter, bought,* etc
/ay/ as in *pay, tail, major,* etc

/e/ as in *bed, said, breath*, etc

/ee/ as in *feel, real, field*, etc

/eer/ as in *beer, mere, hear*, etc

/i/ as in *bit, damage, hymn*, etc

/ie/ as in *tie, high, site*, etc

/ire/ as in *fire, fiery, tyre*, etc

/o/ as in *on, stock, bureaucracy*, etc

/oh/ as in *oh, sew, road*, etc

/oo/ as in *book, full, bosom*, etc

/ooh/ as in *boot, cute, new*, etc

/oor/ as in *boor, tour, cure*, etc

/ow/ as in *owl, about, plough*, etc

/our/ as in *our, tower, sauerkraut*, etc

/oy/ as in *boy, voyage, avoid*, etc

/u/ as in *nut, ton, country*, etc

/ur/ as in *fur, earn, word*, etc

/ə/ as in *ago, father, fluent*, etc

Consonant sounds

As with the vowels, the following list includes sounds, and distinctions between sounds, that are not found in all accents of English.

/b/ as in *book, pebble, rub*, etc

/ch/ as in *cheap, much, cello*, etc

/d/ as in *dog, muddle, end*, etc

/dh/ as in *the, father, soothe*, etc

/f/ as in *fat, laugh, photo*, etc

/g/ as in *give, ghost, egg*, etc

/h/ as in *hat, ahoy, who*, etc

/j/ as in *jeep, budge, agile*, etc

/k/ as in *keep, cat, chasm, queen*, etc

/kh/ as in Scottish *loch*, etc

/l/ as in *leap, film, metal*, etc

/m/ as in *man, film, comb*, etc

/n/ as in *net, mental, ton*, etc

/ng/ as in *sing, think, hungry*, etc

/p/ as in *pot, open, hop*, etc

/r/ as in *rub, currant, rhyme*, etc

/s/ as in *sit, scene, cell*, etc

/sh/ as in *she, machine, nation*, etc

/t/ as in *toe, butter, night*, etc

/th/ as in *thing, breath, panther*, etc

/v/ as in *very, every, of*, etc

/w/ as in *wild, quite, one*, etc

/wh/ as in *why, whistle, white,* etc

/y/ as in *yes, euro, utopia,* etc

/z/ as in *zoo, as, cheese,* etc

/zh/ as in *beige, pleasure, vision,* etc

Stressed syllables are indicated by a stress mark (')
before the stressed syllable: *ma'chine* /mə'sheen/.

Acknowledgements

All the writers listed in the Bibliography (page 307) have contributed in some way to this book, even where I have disagreed with their recommendations and/or explanations. Particular mention must be made of Edward Carney's comprehensive *Survey of English Spelling*, to which I owe the insights underlying the rules outlined on pages 134 and 168.

I would also like to thank Mark Handsley for his many helpful comments on an earlier draft of this book.

Text from *Winnie-the-Pooh* by A A Milne copyright © The Trustees of the Pooh Properties, reproduced by permission of the Curtis Brown Group Ltd, London.

Quotation from George Bernard Shaw reproduced by permission of The Society of Authors, on behalf of the Bernard Shaw Estate.

Text from *What a Word!* by A P Herbert reproduced by permission of A P Watt Ltd on behalf of The Estate of Jocelyn Herbert and The Executors of the Estate of Teresa E Perkins.

1

How to improve your spelling

. . . it has the words DON'T PANIC printed in large friendly letters on its cover.

Douglas Adams, *The Restaurant at the End of the Universe*

Perhaps, like *The Hitch Hiker's Guide to the Galaxy*, every guide to English spelling ought to have DON'T PANIC written in large, friendly letters on its cover. Because even if you have struggled with spelling for years and still consider the rules of English spelling to be almost incomprehensible, there is no need to panic. Just remember *three important things*:

1. English spelling is not nearly as unsystematic and unpredictable as it may seem – there *are* rules and patterns that can be learned, and this book will explain them to you.

2. You already know a lot more about English spelling

than you perhaps realize, and you can build on that knowledge.

3. If you use the tips and techniques described in this chapter and the information provided in the other chapters of this book, **your spelling *will* improve**.

Nine key ways to improve your spelling

1. Learn the rules and regular forms before tackling the exceptions and irregularities

Get to grips with the *regular* spelling patterns first, before you tackle the exceptions and the problem spellings. This is probably the number-one technique for improving your spelling.

Poor spellers often have little grasp of the rules and regularities of English spelling. They see words like *offering* and *referring*, *accommodate* and *accumulate*, *readable* and *legible*, *compromise* and *criticize*, and so on, and though they can see the problems well enough, they cannot see the patterns. Not knowing the rules that explain these spellings, they have to rely on remembering the correct spelling of each word individually, and therefore often make unnecessary and easily avoidable mistakes.

Once you understand the rules, you can more easily spot (and remember) words that are exceptions to these rules. You may even find that apparent exceptions to rules are actually governed by other rules you hadn't been aware of before. But if you don't get a firm grasp of the rules in the first place, you will never see the wood for the trees: you will get completely bogged down and your spelling will never improve.

2. Concentrate on the words you use most often

There are many words in English that have bizarre, unpredictable spellings. You will find many of them in this book. But you don't have to know how to spell them all, or at least not straight away. If you are a poor speller, it makes no sense to worry about the spelling of *chrysanthemum*, *pterodactyl* or *xenophobia* until you have got to grips with *accommodation*, *collaborate* and *vehicle*. Focus your attention on everyday words first.

3. Make a spelling book

Make a spelling notebook (or open a spelling file on your computer).

- Keep a list of the words you know you make mistakes with. (For a start, you could check the lists of common errors in Chapters 3, 4 and 5 and note down the ones you know *you* get wrong (or might get wrong), or check the lists of words with silent letters in Chapter 10.) From now on, every time you come across a word whose spelling you are not quite certain about, or one that you find you have misspelt, add it to your list.
- When you are reading, be on the lookout for words that you might find hard to spell, or whose spellings you find surprising, and note them down in your spelling book.

> **DON'T COPY OTHER PEOPLE'S MISTAKES**
> If you see a word that isn't spelt the way you would
> have expected it to be, don't just assume that it is you
> who are wrong. Other people can make mistakes too.
> Always check the correct spelling of a word in a
> dictionary before you write it into your spelling book.
> (Later in this chapter, there are some comments on
> how to choose and use a dictionary.)

- When you are learning spelling rules, include them
  in your spelling book too. Study the rules in this
  book, then *write them down* in your spelling file.
  Look for examples of words that follow the rules,
  and write them into the file. Look for examples of
  words that *don't* follow the rules, and include them
  too. (For example, you might make a list of verbs
  that can end in -*ise* but not -*ize*.)
- Sometimes you will come across spelling problems
  that are difficult to deal with by a rule. The spellings
  of many words simply have to be learned without
  the aid of a rule (words that end in a silent *b*, for
  example, such as *climb*, *comb*, *crumb*, *lamb*, or *nouns*
  that end in *ar* rather than *er*, such as *liar* and *burglar*).

  If there is no clear rule that you can learn, then
  just make a list of the words. If you gather words
  together in this way, you will more easily remember
  which words belong to the group.

DON'T COPY OUT INCORRECT SPELLINGS
It is *not* a good idea to note incorrect spellings of
words in your spelling file. You need to fix the *correct*
spelling of a word in your mind, not an incorrect one.
As far as possible, get incorrect spellings out of your
mind from now on, and concentrate on the correct
spellings.

4. Check your work

Know your weak points. Always check your work carefully and look for the mistakes you know you are liable
to make. (It is a good idea to read over your spelling
book or spelling file from time to time in order to
remind yourself of the errors you often make or have
made in the past.)

Do not rely on the spellchecker on your computer
(if you have one). A spellchecker is a useful tool, and
one you should certainly make use of, but it has its
limitations:

- A spellchecker is only as good as the list of words it
  has in its data file. If you key in a word that is not
  in the spellchecker file, it will flag it up as incorrect
  even if you have spelt it correctly. (And do check
  that your spellchecker is set for *British* English, not
  American English.)
- A spellchecker can only tell you that you have keyed
  in a sequence of letters that is not in its file of
  acceptable forms. It is therefore much better at indicating accidental keyboarding errors (for example

croase for *coarse*) than many common spelling errors (such as *course* for *coarse*). Since both *coarse* and *course* are acceptable words, the spellchecker cannot indicate the incorrect use of one word for the other: it is *you* who will have to check your use of *coarse* or *course*. (The same applies to *their/there*, *its/it's* and *who's/whose*, and other frequently confused words. See Chapter 5.)

- Although a spellchecker will often flag up your key-boarding errors, it will of course not do so if what you have typed is an acceptable word. It will not, for example, indicate that you have typed *form* instead of *from* or *causal* instead of *casual*. Here again, it is you who will have to check.

And in any case, you may not always have access to a spellchecker. That's why you need to learn to spell.

5. Use memory aids

A 'memory aid' (often called a 'mnemonic') is a word, phrase or rhyme that helps you to remember some-thing (in this case, how to spell correctly). Some spell-ing mnemonics are well known, such as the rule '*i* before *e* except after *c*' which explains the spellings of words such as *field*, *fierce* and *siege* with *ie* and *ceiling* and *deceit* with *ei*.

- You can make up mnemonics for yourself (and it doesn't matter how silly they are as long as they help you to spell correctly). For example, you can remind yourself that there are two *r*'s in *embarrass* if you remember that you might go *really red* with *embar-rassment*; if you have difficulty remembering the position of the *a*'s and the *e* in *calendar*, remember that a *calendar* (-*a-e-a*-) shows the days of *a year* (-*a-e-a*-); you wouldn't *deign* to do something that was beneath your *dignity*; and if something is *ghastly*, it's *horrible* (it would be pretty *horrible* to see a *ghost* as well).

- A mnemonic might even be a picture you have in your mind, related in some way to the word you want to spell. For example, if you want to remember that there are two *g*'s in *aggressive*, you could have a mental picture of two *gorillas* fighting. And if you want to remember the double *s* as well, you could think of the two gorillas wearing *silk scarves*. (Yes, of course it's silly, but it works, and anything that works is worth doing.) Similarly, you could imagine that a *leopard* in a *leotard* might be in *jeopardy*.

  This technique is particularly useful for reminding you of the spellings of words that just don't seem to fit into any pattern and that you keep on having problems with. You don't need a pattern or a rule, you just need a picture.

Memory aids provided in this book are marked with the symbol ★. Don't forget to write the memory aids into your spelling book along with the words they help you to spell.

6. Use word-families as a spelling aid
One of the many problems in English spelling is the existence of 'silent letters', letters that are written but not pronounced (such as the *w* of *written*, for example). In many cases there are no clues to the

presence of such silent letters, but fortunately there are sometimes related words that *do* provide useful reminders. For example, although the *g* is silent in *sign* and *resign*, it is pronounced in the related words *signature* and *resignation*. Similarly, the word *autumnal* reminds us that there is a silent *n* at the end of *autumn*, and for those who do not pronounce the *n* in the middle of *government*, the verb *govern* is a reminder of the *n* that must be written.

Take another example: words such as *intelligence* and *vigilance*. The endings of these words sound the same, so how do you know whether to write an *e* or an *a*? Here again, related words in the word-families can come to your rescue: for example, the *e* is clearly pronounced in *intelligentsia*, and the *a* in *vigilante*. The same holds true for *essence* and *essential*, *parent* and *parental*, *providence* and *providential*, *existence* and *existentialism*, *torrent* and *torrential*, *substance* and *substantial*, *grammar* and *grammatical*, and *ignorance* and *ignoramus*.

Word-families also help you with the problem of deciding whether there should be a single or double letter in a word:

crime, criminal	*sane, sanity*
omen, ominous	*obscene, obscenity*
extreme, extremity	

So by looking at words in families, you can use the clear and obvious spelling of one word to help you deal with the doubtful spelling of another. Word-families like these are another useful thing to add to your spelling file.

How far you can stretch the concept of word-family depends, of course, on your knowledge of English (and your use of a dictionary – a dictionary is a useful tool for finding word-families, as related words will often be found close to one another). Meaning can often be a clue as well: while not everyone would necessarily see the family connection between *doubt* and *dubious*, their meanings are clearly related, and so the *b* of *dubious* can be a reminder of the *b* of *doubt*.

7. Break words up into parts

Many people make mistakes in spelling simply because they do not look closely enough (if at all) at the *structure* of the words they are writing.

- Breaking words up into their component parts will often help you avoid spelling errors.

    For example, you know that *unnecessary* means 'not necessary', *illegal* means 'not legal' and *dissimilar* means 'not similar': the structure of these words is clearly *un - necessary*, *il - legal* and *dis - similar*. So you obviously need two *n*'s, two *l*'s and two *s*'s and there is no excuse for writing ✗*unecessary*, ✗*ilegal* or ✗*disimilar*.

    The same principle applies to words ending in *-ly*, such as *really* and *actually*. The structure of these words is obviously *real - ly* and *actual - ly*, so there must be two *l*'s in each word, not just one (a very common error). And the same goes for words like *drunkenness*, *keenness* and *suddenness*, which need two *n*'s: *drunken - ness*, *keen - ness*, *sudden - ness*, not ✗*drunkeness*, etc.

On the other hand, to *disappear* is to *dis - appear*, the opposite of *appear*; so you only need one *s*, not two (another common error). The same is true for *disappoint*, the structure of which is *dis - appoint*. (In modern English the connection between *appoint* and *disappoint* is not obvious, but originally 'disappointing' someone meant the opposite of appointing them – which goes to show that a little knowledge of word origins can also be a useful spelling aid.)

- Many technical words in English have come into the language from Latin and Greek, or have been created using elements taken from Latin and Greek (such as *photo-*, *hydro-*, *aero-*, *physio-*, *psycho-*, *-phobia* and *-lysis*). Learning to recognize these Latin and Greek elements (see Chapter 9) and how to spell them correctly is another useful spelling technique.

  If, for example, you know that many words that have to do with thinking or the mind have an element in them that comes from Greek and is written *psych*, then you are already well on the way to spelling all such words correctly with a *p*, a *y* and a *ch*.

- In words derived from Latin, you can often recognize elements that crop up in many different words, such as the *fer* of *conference*, *deference*, *difference*, *inference*, *interference*, *preference*, *reference* and *transference*. This can help with the problems of spelling word-endings correctly: notice that all these *fer* words end in *-ence*, not *-ance*.

- Even simply saying a word slowly to yourself so that each syllable is sounded separately (e.g. *com-pu-ter*, *na-tu-ral, re-la-tion*) is a good way of checking your spelling.

8. Take an interest in word-origins

You may think that the origins of words, their *etymologies*, are of no concern to you (all you want to do is spell correctly), but looking at the origins of words in your dictionary at the same time as checking their spellings often makes it clear why the words are spelt the way they are, and if you know *why* a word is spelt as it is, you will all the more easily remember how to spell it.

Disappoint, mentioned above, is one example of this. Another example is *Mediterranean*, which comes from two Latin words *medius* 'middle' (the root of English *medium*) and *terra* 'land' (which underlies English *terrace, terrain, terrestrial* and *territory*): for the Romans, the Mediterranean Sea was 'the sea in the middle of the land' as it is almost completely surrounded by land. Any time you come to write *Mediterranean*, this information will come back into your mind and will help you remember how to spell the word correctly.

It will often be useful to add some brief details of word-origins to your spelling book or spelling file beside the words whose spellings they explain.

9. Practise

And lastly, *practise*. It isn't enough just to check your spelling when you happen to be writing something (though it is certainly important that you *do* always check your spelling at such times). Set aside some time every day to work specifically on spelling. For example, look at your spelling book or spelling file regularly and remind yourself of what you have learned. Note anything that you are still not quite sure about and work on it until you are sure.

- One technique that is used in many schools is **look–spell–write–check**: look carefully at the word you are learning (make sure you are starting off with the correct spelling) and spell it out loud; cover the word over and then write it out (you can spell it out loud again as you write it); then uncover the original word and check your spelling.

- Another useful exercise is to write down ten words every day that you know you often get wrong, and check that you are now spelling them correctly. Remind yourself of any spelling rules you have applied in writing these words, and then think of other words that follow the same rules. Even if there aren't any rules, remind yourself of other words that belong in the same group (for example, words such as *pneumonia* that begin with a silent *p*, words such as *survivor* and *visitor* that have *or* where you might expect *er*, or words that have the sound /f/ written as *ph*).

In spelling, as in so many other skills, practice *does* make perfect.

> *Summary of key points*
> - Concentrate first on the regular forms rather than the exceptions, and on everyday words rather than rare and obscure ones.
> - Make a spelling book or spelling file.
> - Use memory aids, word-families and word origins to help you spell correctly.
> - Break words up into their component parts and check that each part is spelt correctly.
> - Always check your work carefully and look out for the errors you know you are liable to make.
> - Practise spelling every day.

Choosing and using a dictionary

Choosing a dictionary

You are going to be making a two-pronged attack on your spelling problems. With this book, you will be guided through the difficulties of English spelling, gaining an understanding of the rules and an awareness of the exceptions. But you will also need to use a dictionary regularly, to check up on the spellings of words that, owing to the necessarily limited space available, have had to be omitted from the various word lists in this book. So, first things first – make sure you have a good, up-to-date dictionary.

You will have to decide for yourself what size of dictionary you want, so before making up your mind, have a careful look at all the dictionaries on the shelves of a good bookshop. Remember that if the dictionary you choose is too small, it won't have all the words in it that you need to check, so it is probably safer always to choose one that is larger than you think you need.

Look at the pages of the dictionaries you are considering buying. Do you find them easy to read? Try searching for some words that you know you misspell. Is it easy to find the words you are looking for? Choose a dictionary you are comfortable with, one that you will enjoy using, and don't forget that you will need to use it not just for checking spelling but also for checking the meanings of words (to ensure that the word you are spelling is actually the correct word to express what you want to say) and their origins as well.

Consulting a dictionary

Some people find dictionaries off-putting and difficult to use, but there is no reason why this should be so. All that you need to know is how words are listed in a dictionary, and more importantly how they are listed in *your* dictionary, since not all dictionaries use the same system.

In all dictionaries, the main words (known as *headwords*) are listed in alphabetical order and are generally in heavy black **boldface** type so that they stand out on the page. The paragraph of information that follows each headword is known as an *entry*.

In many dictionaries, most words, including compounds, are treated as headwords and are given a separate entry. For example:

big	**big cat**
bigamy	**big game**

bighead	big time
bight	big top
bigmouth	bigwig
bigot	

Some of these words may have related words within their entries. For example, in the entry for **big**, you might also find words such as **biggish** and **bigness**, in the entry for **bigamy** you might also find **bigamist** and **bigamous**, and in the entry for **bighead** you might also find **bigheaded** and **bigheadedness**, and so on. (Words like **biggish**, **bigamous** and **bigheaded** are known as *derivatives*.)

The words that you would find in the entries for the above headwords might therefore be:

big	bigmouth
biggish, bigness	*bigmouthed*
bigamy	bigot
bigamist, bigamous	*bigoted, bigotry*
big cat	big time
big game	*big-timer*
bighead	big top
bigheaded, bigheadedness	bigwig
bight	

The only problem that arises with this system is that you would not find the word **biggish** in its alphabetical position between **big game** and **bighead**, but only listed under the headword **big**. But this is really not much of a problem at all once you realize that this is the system your dictionary uses.

In other dictionaries, the compound words, such as

big cat, big game and **bighead**, are not given separate entries but are listed within the entry for the word that is the first part of the compound, in this case **big**. These compound words usually follow the derivatives. In dictionaries of this type, therefore, there are fewer headwords and more words listed within the entries:

big

  biggish, bigness

  big cat, big game, bighead, bigheaded, bigheadedness, big-mouth, bigmouthed, big time, big-timer, big top, bigwig

bigamy

  bigamist, bigamous

bight

bigot

  bigoted, bigotry

If you have a dictionary of this type, there is again no problem at all once you understand the system and therefore know where to look for a word.

One other point to note about dictionaries is that *homonyms* (different words with the same spelling) are usually given separate entries in dictionaries. So, for example, **bit** = a small part, **bit** = a unit of computer information, **bit** = part of a horse's bridle, and **bit** = the past tense of *bite* will generally be found in four separate entries in a dictionary. And note also that in some dictionaries related verbs and nouns (such as *to buy something* and *a good buy*), related adjectives and nouns (such as *a red box* and *in the red*), and so on, will have separate entries, while in other dictionaries they will be found together in one single entry.

But whatever system your own dictionary uses, once

you understand it, you will very quickly find your way around when looking for words. In short, it doesn't matter which type of dictionary you buy so long as you know how to use it and are comfortable with it.

How to find a word you can't spell

But, of course, for poor spellers a major difficulty is: how do you find a word if you don't know how to spell it? If, for example, you were to look up *✗acomodation* in a dictionary when you were trying to check the spelling of *accommodation*, you wouldn't find the word you wanted because you would probably be looking on the wrong page. Similarly, you wouldn't find *mnemonic* or *pneumonia* at N or *pterodactyl* at T.

So how *do* you find a word if you are not sure how to spell it? It's simple – you use the information in this book to guide you. Odd as English spelling sometimes is, there are nevertheless only a limited number of ways a word could be spelt, and by the time you have studied this book, you will know what they are. For example:

- In Chapters 6 and 7, you can familiarize yourself with the unexpected ways in which the sounds of English are represented in writing. Chapter 9, which covers word-elements such as *aero-*, would obviously also be of help here.
- The sections of Chapter 7 in which the rules governing spellings with single and double letters are explained would get you over the *✗acomodation* hurdle, because you would expect a double *c* and a double *m* in a word that ends in *-ation* (and you would know why).

- The *Index of difficult words* on page 309 includes common misspellings of words, along with their correct spellings. Search here if you cannot find a word you are looking for in a dictionary – it may be that you are looking for the word in the wrong place.

Summary of key points

- Choose a dictionary that you find easy to use and that is big enough to have all the words you are likely to look up.
- Get to know the structure of your dictionary, so that you know how to find words quickly.
- Familiarize yourself with the chapters of this book that deal with silent letters and double letters, so that you are not confused by unexpected spellings.

2

1066 and other bits of history

. . . English speech, the sea which receives tributaries from every region under heaven.

Ralph Waldo Emerson

The origins of present-day English spelling

If William the Conqueror had *lost* the Battle of Hastings, English today might well be a language not unlike Dutch, and English spelling would almost certainly be a lot easier than it is.

It is not the purpose of this book to look in any great detail at the history and development of English spelling, because as someone who has difficulty with spelling, you are obviously not so much concerned with how English spelling got into its current state as with finding ways of coping with it as it is today. But as you have already seen in Chapter 1, some knowledge of word-origins and of how present-day English spelling arose can actually be of great help in learning to spell correctly, and recognizing that an English word has come into the language from, say, Latin or Greek can actually help you remember how to spell it. So a brief look at how modern English spelling has developed over the years is not out of place in a spelling book.

So, briefly, how *has* English spelling developed into what it is today? Well, it has taken over 15 centuries of history, involving (among other things) invasions by Germanic tribes in the fifth and sixth centuries and by the Vikings a few centuries later, a major regime change in 1066, extensive changes in English pronunciation in the 15th and 16th centuries, the citizens of London, the printing practices of Dutch printers, the influx of Latin and Greek words into English from the Middle Ages onwards, and more than a little scholarly pedantry.

Let's start at the very beginning . . .
Well, perhaps not at the *very* beginning. That would take us back 6,000 years or more to the nomads of the steppes of southern Russia who spoke a language which, as the nomads spread out from their original homeland, gradually developed into separate languages such as Greek, Latin, Sanskrit, Celtic, Germanic and Hittite.

The road to modern English, however, really begins some 1,500 years ago with a language, known as Old English or Anglo-Saxon, that was brought into this country by the Angles, Saxons and Jutes, Germanic tribes from northern Europe. English therefore belongs to the same family of languages as German and Dutch, its nearest relative being Frisian, which is still spoken in parts of Germany and the Netherlands.

Anglo-Saxon, or Old English, had an alphabet of 27 letters but a sound system of about 40 different speech sounds. Nevertheless, Anglo-Saxon spelling gave a fairly good representation of Anglo-Saxon pronunciation.

The situation did not change much when the Vikings established their separate territory, the Danelaw, in northern and eastern England. Old Norse, the language of the Vikings and the ancestor of present-day Norwegian, Swedish and Danish, was closely related to Anglo-Saxon in any case, and many Old Norse words were introduced into Old English. (*Egg*, *leg*, *sky* and *window*, for example, are from Old Norse, not Anglo-Saxon.)

1066 . . .

Then came the Norman Conquest. The Normans (themselves of Viking origin) spoke a variety of French, which belongs to the Romance family of languages that developed from Latin and are found over much of the territory of the former Roman empire. (Other Romance languages are Italian, Spanish, Portuguese and Romanian.) Norman French was therefore very different from Old English in vocabulary, pronunciation and spelling.

Old English ceased to be a written language in the 12th century, though it continued to be spoken and was greatly influenced by French. When English once again became the language of literature in the 14th century, it was therefore very different from what it had been two or three centuries earlier. Many Anglo-Saxon words had been replaced by French words, many new words of French origin had been introduced into English, and even some of the Anglo-Saxon words that remained in the language had been respelt according to French spelling rules. For example, the French scribes introduced the spelling *qu* as a replacement for Old English *cw* (Old English *cwen, cwellan, cwic*; modern English *queen, quell, quick*).

Norman French differed in spelling and pronunciation from Parisian French, which added to the complications. *Gaol*, for example, is a Norman French word but its pronunciation /jayl/ derives from Parisian French (as does the alternative spelling *jail*). It is also to Parisian French that we owe the *gu* spellings of words such as *guard, guarantee* and *guardian* (Norman French gave us *ward, warranty* and *warden*).

It is thus with the arrival of French in Britain that our spelling problems really begin. The development of printing in the 15th and 16th centuries added to the complications, as many early printers were foreign, especially from the Netherlands, and used their own spellings when printing English. (One example of this is the word *ghost*, with a Dutch *gh* where Old English had *g*.)

Changes in English pronunciation

But not all the oddities of modern English spelling can be laid at the door of incomers. There are two other important factors dating from the Middle Ages, both purely English.

Firstly, the speech of London, being the speech of the capital, had a strong influence on the development of English. But the inhabitants of London, coming from many different parts of the country, spoke with many different accents, and this gave rise to some mismatches between sound and spelling. *Bury* and *burial*, for example, were written with the *u* spelling that reflected London pronunciation of the time, but our modern pronunciation of these words derives from the pronunciation of the words as spoken in Kent. Similarly, *one* and *once* have a London-based spelling but an originally non-London pronunciation – *alone* (from *all one*) and *atone* (from *at one*) show the London pronunciation of *one*.

Secondly, there have been huge changes to the pronunciation of English that began in the 15th and 16th centuries, but our writing system has not changed to keep pace with them. The result is again a mismatch between sound and spelling, and many spelling problems. For example, the vowel sounds in words such as *deep* and *deal* were different in the 14th century (more like the vowels of *day* and *dell*). It is only more recently that words like this have come to have the same vowel sound. The spellings, however, have remained as they were, which is why we now have some words with the /ee/ sound spelt *ee* and others spelt *ea*.

And to add to the confusion, some letters, such as the *k* of *know* and *knight* and the *w* of *wrong* and *write*, which were pronounced in Anglo-Saxon, have become silent (that is, are no longer pronounced), but we still have to write them.

Scholarship and pedantry

Many English words have come to us, via French, from Latin, and in the 16th century, there were scholars who thought that the spellings of such words should reflect their Latin origins. For this reason, many silent letters were added to English words at this time. For example, a *b* was added to *dette* (from Latin *debitum*) and to *doute* (from Latin *dubitare*), so saddling us with the modern spellings *debt* and *doubt*. (It was not, of course, being suggested that these letters should be *pronounced*, merely that they should be *written*.) Similarly, some words of Greek origin were given a new spelling that reflected their Greek origins: *rime* became *rhyme* (compare *rhythm*, which comes from the same Greek word *rhythmos*) and *abyss* and *abysm*, previously spelt with an *i*, gained a *y* spelling to reflect the Greek word *abyssos* from which they are both derived.

Worse still, the scholars and dictionary-writers were not always careful to be consistent in their application of this principle, and that is why we have such spellings as *receipt* (with a silent *p* that reflects Latin *receptum*) but *deceit* and *conceit* without *p* (although derived from Latin *deceptum* and *conceptum*), and similarly *deign* but *disdain* (both ultimately from Latin *dignus*).

Occasionally, scholars got things completely wrong and introduced spellings that had no justification whatsoever. For example, there is today an *s* in *island* because the word was thought to be related to Latin *insula*; actually it comes from Anglo-Saxon *iegland* (although *isle* comes, via French, from *insula*). *Scythe* (from Old English *sithe*) gained an extra *c* because of a supposed connection with Latin *scindere* 'to cut', and *scissors* (from

Latin *cisoria*) gained an *s* for the same reason. And it was not just Latinized spellings that were introduced: the *ptarmigan*, whose name comes from Gaelic *tarmachan*, gained an initial silent *p* that rightly only belongs to pterodactyls and pterosaurs (Greek *pteron* 'a wing').

The current situation

Given the history of the language, it is hardly surprising that English spelling has developed into the confused and confusing state we find it in today. But it is not the case, as many people believe, that there is *no* system to English spelling; it is, rather, that English spelling comprises *several different spelling systems* mixed together – for example, the one that derives from Anglo-Saxon that gives us many of our common spellings but also some of our silent letters, the one that derives from Latin (often influenced by French) that has many of the double-letter spellings that give rise to so many errors, and the one that derives from Greek that has given us such difficult and unpredictable spellings as *physics*, *psychology*, *diarrhoea* and *catarrh*.

In addition, English has adopted words from many other languages which have quite different spelling systems, and in many cases has kept the foreign spellings. This has inevitably added to the confusion. For example, while in Italian there is nothing odd about using *gh* to spell the sound /g/ of *spaghetti* or *ghetto*, *gh* is not a normal way of spelling /g/ in English. A little piece of the regular Italian spelling system has been incorporated into English spelling, where it is completely irregular. Similarly, it is only in words that have come into English from French that we spell the

/sh/ sound with *ch*, as in *machine* and *moustache*. A perfectly regular French spelling has been brought into English, where it is yet one more irregularity that has to be learned.

Spelling the /k/ sound

A look at some of the different ways in which the sound /k/ is spelt in modern English gives a good indication of the complexity of English spelling and how our spelling has been made even more complicated by words and spellings from other languages.

From Old English or Middle English:
can, carve, cold, comb, cow, crib, cut, scrap, screech
bleak, keep, king, kiss, make, skin, speak, think, wrinkle, yolk
back, black, knuckle, sack, stick, thick, tickle
box, fox, six
ache

With the *qu* spelling introduced by the Anglo-Norman scribes:
queen, quick, squeak, squeal, squeeze

From Greek:
disk, kilo, kleptomania, krypton, leukaemia, plankton, skeleton
architect, chaos, Christmas, monarch, psychic, scheme, school, stomach, technical
academy, cycle, disc, eclipse, ecstasy, eczema, sceptic
climax, lexical, orthodox, oxygen
saccharine

From Latin (often via French):

accommodate, occupy, occur, succumb
accident, eccentric, succeed, vaccine
exceed, except, excite
liquid, oblique

From French:

bloc, chic, cognac, sac, tic, traffic
bouquet, grotesque, liqueur, liquor, mosque, quiche, unique
lacquer

From Italian:

fiasco, macaroni, pizzicato, portico
broccoli, piccolo, staccato, toccata
scherzo
zucchini

From Spanish:

peccadillo
mosquito

From German:

blitzkrieg, flak, kaput, sauerkraut

From Arabic:

alchemy
alcohol, alcove
alkali, Koran (or Qur'an)
qadi

From Hindi and Urdu:

gymkhana, khaki
pukka

From various other languages:
*amok, kayak, kapok, kiosk, trek, wok, yak
khan*

So while you might have thought that, as a poor speller, you have problems enough with present-day English and have no need to concern yourself with the history of the language, you can perhaps now see that it is not so. While it may still be difficult to master a spelling system that includes the Anglo-Saxon *ch* of *chin* and *church*, the Greek *ch* of *chaos* and *chasm* and the French *ch* of *chic* and *charade*, understanding something of the origins and development of our English vocabulary and spelling can actually be a useful aid in learning to spell. It will often give you a 'hook' to hang a difficult spelling on in your mind or a 'label' to remember it by.

But even if that is no consolation to you, at least you now know who to blame for your problems!

Summary of key points

- Modern English spelling is a mixture of spelling systems deriving from several different languages.
- English pronunciation has changed over the years, but English spelling does not reflect many of these changes.
- Knowing what language a word comes from can often help you remember an unexpected or difficult spelling.

3
Frequently misspelt words

English spelling would seem to have been designed chiefly as a disguise for pronunciation.

Jerome K Jerome

Of course, the problem with English spelling is that, for the most part, it hasn't been designed at all. It has developed haphazardly, and over the years has incorporated several different spelling systems (Anglo-Saxon, Latin, Greek, French, Italian, Arabic, . . .).

And just as spelling may disguise pronunciation, pronunciation is often not a reliable guide to spelling. (If it was, you wouldn't need this book.) The mismatch between pronunciation and spelling in English is precisely what makes for so many spelling problems and spelling mistakes.

How to use this chapter

- You will find here a list of the most frequently misspelt words, with the most frequently misspelt parts of the words highlighted in *italic* type. You should read through this list carefully, checking that you are sure of all the spellings (perhaps by using the **look–spell–write–check** method described on page 12). Any words that you spell incorrectly or are not sure of should be added to your spelling book or spelling file.

- As can be seen from a glance down the columns of words on pages 32–49, a large proportion of the errors listed here are due to a lack of understanding of only a *very few* basic rules, especially those governing the choice between *-able* and *-ible* (e.g. *abominable* and *irresistible*); *-ance* and *-ence* (e.g. *extravagance* and *correspondence*); *-er*, *-or* and *-ar* (as in *lender*, *visitor* and *burglar*); and single and double letters (as in *preference* and *occurrence*). For that reason, many of the entries in this chapter, in addition to giving you the correct spellings, also include cross-references to the pages where the spelling rules are explained.

    You should, therefore, not only check through this chapter for words that you spell (or might spell) incorrectly, but also look up the relevant sections of the book to make sure that you understand the underlying rules. This will make it much easier to learn and remember the correct spellings. You should add both the words and the rules to your spelling file.

- Where no rule can be given for a particular spelling, it is often possible to make up a mnemonic (or memory aid) to help you, or it may be that there are other members of the word-family that provide a clue. Many of the entries in the following list therefore include simple mnemonics or references to related words that may help you remember the correct spelling. These are marked with the symbol ★. (Try making up other mnemonics for yourself – ones you make up yourself may be even easier to remember than the ones already supplied in this book.)

  The mnemonics and word-families should be added to your spelling file along with the words they refer to.

- A useful aid to spelling words of, say, French or Greek origin, is to *name* the unexpected spellings. So, for example, we could call the *y* of *abyss* and *abysmal* the 'Greek *y*' or 'Greek /i/', the *ch* of *character* the 'Greek *ch*' or 'Greek /k/', the *ch* of *chic* the 'French *ch*' or 'French /sh/', and so on. Giving these difficult spellings labels is a way of fixing them in your head. (Your dictionary will tell you what languages these difficult spellings come from.)

American English
Remember that American English spells many words differently from British English (see Chapter 18). In American books and magazines, therefore, you may see some of the words in this list spelt differently from the way they are here. They are not wrong, they are just not correct in *British* English.

---

abandoned
  n – page 150
abbreviate, abbreviation
  bb – page 161
aberration
  b – page 162;
  ★ *err* as in *to err*
abhorrence, abhorrent
  ★ related to *horrid*;
  ence – page 181
abominable
  ★ related word *ominous*;
  able – page 174
abscess
  ★ an *abscess* is *pus* in a *cavity*
abysmal, abyss
  both words have the *y* that can be thought of as 'Greek /i/'
accelerate, accelerator
  cc – page 161;
  l – page 162;
  or – page 191
accessible
  cc – page 161;
  ible – page 174

accessory
  cc – page 161;
  ory – page 187
accidentally
  = *accidental* - *ly*;
  cc – page 161
accommodate, accommodation
  cc – page 161;
  mm – page 161
accompany, accompaniment
  cc – page 161;
  o – page 116;
  y to *i* – page 120
accomplish
  cc – page 161;
  o – page 116
accumulate, accumulation
  cc – page 161;
  m – page 162
accuracy, accurate
  cc – page 161;
  r – page 162;
  acy, ate – page 180
accustomed
  cc – page 161;
  m – page 150

acknowledge
★ related to *know*, but remember the *c*;
dge – page 166

acquaint, acquaintance
cq – page 162;
ance – page 181

acquiesce, acquiescent
cq – page 162;
esc – page 220;
ent – page 186

acquire, acquisition, acquisitive
cq – page 162;
★ for *acquisition*, remember *acquire*;
★ for *acquisitive*, think of *acquisition*

acquit, acquittal
cq – page 162;
tt – page 150

across
★ to go *across* a river is to *cross* it

actually
= *actual* - *ly*

additional
★ related to the verb *add*

address
★ an *address* is something you *add* to an envelope

adequacy, adequate
★ related to *equal*;
acy – page 180;
ate – page 180

admission, admitted, admittance
tt – page 150;

ance – page 181
not *add* – page 161

adolescence, adolescent
esc – page 220;
en – page 181

advantageous
eous – page 197

advertise, advertisement
ise – page 198

aggravate, aggravation
gg – page 161

aggression, aggressive
gg – page 161

aghast
★ spelling influenced by *ghost*

agree
★ he *agreed* not to be *greedy*

align, alignment
★ *gee*, what an odd spelling!

allege, allegation
ll – page 163;
★ for *allege*, think of *allegation*

allotment, allotted
tt – page 150

amateur
' "French" *eur*', as also in *chauffeur, entrepreneur,* etc;
not ✗ *-ure*

amount
★ how much does a *mountain amount* to?

annihilate
nn – page 161;
★ *nihil* is Latin for 'nothing'

announce, announcement
nn – page 163

annul, annulment
  nn – page 163;
  l – page 138
anoint
  only one n
anonymous
  nym – page 224
answer
  ★ related to swear
Antarctic
  ★ it's cold in the Antarctic
apology
  ★ he made a polite
  apology
appal, appalling
  pp – page 163;
  l, ll – page 153
apparatus
  pp – page 163
apparent
  pp – page 161;
  ent – page 186
appear, appearance
  pp – page 163;
  ance – page 181
appreciate
  pp – page 161
appropriate
  pp – page 161
  ate – page 180
approve, approval
  pp – page 163
aquarium
  ★ there was a queer fish in
  the aquarium
arbitrary
  ★ related word arbitration

Arctic
  ★ it's cold in the Arctic
argue, argument
  loss of e – page 104
arthritis
  itis – page 222
asphyxiate, asphyxiation
  ph = 'Greek /f/' and y =
  'Greek /i/'
aspirin
assassin, assassinate,
  assassination
assignment
  ss – page 163;
  ★ for the silent g, think of
  assignation
assimilate
  ss – page 161;
  ★ simil as in similar
assistance, assistant
  ss – page 163;
  an – page 181
associate
  ss – page 161
asthma
atrocious
attach, attachment
  tt – page 163;
  ch – page 127
attendant
  tt – page 163;
  ant – page 186
attitude
  tt – page 163
autumn
  ★ related word
  autumnal

aw*fully*
= *awful - ly*

ba**ch**elor
ch – page 125

ba**gg**age
gg – page 149

barbe*cue*

basic*ally*
ally – page 202

b*eau*tiful
★ related word *beau*

begi**nn**er, begi**nn**ing
nn – page 150

b*ei*ge
a French word

bel*ief*, bel*ie*ve
ie – page 107

bene**f**icial
★ related word *benevolent*

bene**f**it, bene**f**ited
★ related word *benevolent*;
t – page 150

bia**s**ed
s – page 148

billio**n**aire
single *n*

bla**n**cmange
a French word

bour*geois*
a French word; the *s* is
heard in *bourgeoisie*

bro**cc**oli
★ *broccoli* is related to
cabbages and cauliflowers

bro**ch**ure
'French *ch*'

bu**ll**e**t**in

buoy, buo**y**ancy, buoyant
an – page 181;
★ Americans pronounce
buoy /'booh-ee/

bur*eau*cra*c*y, bureaucratic
★ related word *bureau;*
acy – page 180

business
★ *business* keeps you *busily*
occupied

ca**l**endar
★ a *calendar* shows the days
of *a year*

camou**f**lage
a French word

campa**ig**n

ca**nn**abis

care**er**

care**ss**

ca**rr**iage
= *carry* + word-ending *age*

cas**u**al, cas**u**alty
!! do not confuse *casual* and
causal

cata**rrh**
rrh – page 226

cha**ll**enge

champagne
a French word with French
spelling

change**a**ble
ea – page 176

character, characteristic*ally*
'Greek *ch*';
ally – page 202

ch*ief*, ch*ie*fly
ie – page 107

chocolate
*chr*ysanthemum

> . . . *that which we call a rose*
> *By any other name would smell as*
> *sweet.*
> William Shakespeare, *Romeo and Juliet*
>
> *A chrysanthemum by any other*
> *name would be easier to spell.*
> William J Johnston, *Reader's Digest*

circ*u*it
  needs the *u* to make the
  letter c sound as /k/, as also
  in *biscuit*
colla*b*orate, colla*b*orator
  ★ related word *laborious*;
  ll – page 162;
  or – page 192
colla*p*se, colla*p*s*i*ble
  ll – page 162;
  ible – page 174
coll*e*ague
  ll – page 163
coll*e*ge
  ll – page 163;
  !! watch the ending *ege* –
  page 135
colo*ss*al
  ★ the business made a
  colossal loss
colum*n*
  ★ related word *columnist*
comm*e*morate
  ★ related word *memory*;
  mm – page 162

com*mit*ment, com*mitt*ed,
  committee
  mm –page 163;
  t, tt – page 150
compar*a*tive, comparison
compat*i*ble
  ible – page 174
compe*t*ent
  ★ related to *compete*;
  ent – page 186
competition, competi*t*ive,
  competit*or*
  the pronunciations of
  competition and *competitive*
  together show clearly the *e*
  and *i* spellings;
  or – page 192
con*c*ede
  cede – page 218
conc*ei*ve, conc*ei*t,
  conc*ei*ted
  ei – page 107
condem*n*
  ★ related word
  condemnation
conference
  r – page 152;
  ence – page 181
con*n*ection
  nn – page 161;
  ct – page 212
con*n*oisseur
  the spelling is French
con*sci*ence
  ★ related to *conscientious*;
  sci – page 226;
  ence – page 181

conscientious
sci – page 226
conscious
sci – page 226
contemporary
★ related word
contemporaneous
controversial
★ related word
controversy
convalescence, convalescent
esc – page 220;
en – page 181
corollary
correspondence
rr – page 161;
ence – page 181
corroborate, corroboration
rr – page 161
counterfeit
ei – page 107
critically
= *critical - ly*
cupboard
★ originally a *board* or table
for *cups*, etc
curriculum
daily
deceit, deceive
ei – page 107
defence, defensive
c, s – page 125
defendant
ant – page 186
definite, definitely
★ related word *finite*
!! not *definately*,

although some people
pronounce the word
/-aytli/
dependant, dependent
ant for the noun, *ent*
for the adjective –
page 186
descendant
ant – page 186
desiccated
★ often used of coconut: for
spelling, think of *sweet*
coconut
despair
★ related word *desperate*
desperate
★ related word *desperation*
detach
ch – page 125
deterrent
rr – page 152;
ent – page 186
diamond
diaphragm
ph = 'Greek /f/'
★ there is a related
adjective *diaphragmatic*,
in which the *g* is
pronounced
diarrhoea
rrh – page 226
difference, different
ff – page 163;
r – page 152;
en – page 181
★ related word *differential*
dilemma

dile*tt*ante
di*ph*theria
  ph = 'Greek /f/' but
  sometimes pronounced /p/
di*ph*thong
  ph = 'Greek /f/' but
  sometimes pronounced /p/
di*s*a*pp*ear, disappea*r*ance
  = *dis - appear*;
  pp – page 163;
  ance – page 181
di*s*a*pp*oint, disappointment
  = *dis - appoint*;
  pp – page 163
di*s*a*pp*rove, disapproval
  = *dis - approve*;
  pp – page 163
disaster, disa*s*trous
  loss of *e* – page 105
di*s*cipline, di*s*ciplin*a*ry
  ary – page 189
di*s*patch, de*s*patch
  both correct
di*ss*atisfaction, dissatisfied
  = *dis - satisfaction*,
  dis - satisfied
di*ss*ect, dissection
  ss – page 160
di*ss*imilar
  = *dis - similar*
di*ss*ipated, dissipation
  ss – page 160
di*ss*olve
  ss – page 160
do*'s* and don*'ts*
due, d*u*ly
  loss of *e* – page 104

*ea*rnest
*ea*rring
  = *ear - ring*
e*cc*entric
  not *ex* – page 230
e*c*stasy, ecstatic
  not *ex* – page 230
e*c*zema
  not *ex* – page 230
e*ffi*cient, efficiency
  ff – page 163;
  en – page 181;
  cy – page 126
eig*h*t*h*
emba*rr*ass, embarrassment
  ★ you go *really red*
encyclop*ae*dia, encyclop*e*dia
  both correct – page 97
end*eavou*r
  our – page 202
enro*l*, enrolment
  l – page 138
enthusiastic*ally*
  ally – page 202
e*x*aggerate, exaggeration
  ex – page 230
e*x*asperate, exasperation
  ex – page 230
e*x*ceed
  exc – page 230;
  ceed – page 218
e*x*cept
  exc – page 230
e*x*cerpt
  exc – page 230
e*x*citing, excitement
  exc – page 230

exercise
  ex – page 230;
  ise – page 198
exhaust, exhaustion
  exh – page 230
exhibit, exhibition
  exh – page 230;
  ★ related word *inhibit*
exhilarate, exhilaration
  exh – page 230;
  ★ related word *hilarity*
exhort, exhortation
  exh – page 230
existence
  ex – page 230;
  ence – page 181
extraordinary
  ★ = *extra* meaning 'outside'
  + *ordinary*
extravagance, extravagant
  ★ related to *extravaganza*
extrovert, extravert
  both correct
facetious
  ★ *a, e, i, o* and *u* come in
  alphabetical order in this word
fascinate, fascination
favourite
  our – page 202;
February
flotation
fluorescent
  ★ related to *fluoride*, in
  which the *u* is usually
  pronounced;
  esc – page 220;
  ent – page 186

foreign
  ei – page 107
forfeit
  ei – page 107
forgiveness
  logically, you might expect
  two *n*'s here, but there is
  only one
forgo
  for – page 220
forty
friend
  not *ei* – page 107
  ★ *friend* ends in *end*
fulfil, fulfilment; fulfilled
  l, ll – page 153
fundamental
  ★ related to *foundation*
gaiety
gay, gaily
  y to *i* – page 123
gaol
  !! not *goal*
gauge
genealogy
  !! this is not an 'ology'
ghastly
  ★ spelling influenced by *ghost*
government
  ★ related to *govern*
governor
  or – page 191
grammar, grammatical
  grammatical shows the *a* of
  grammar
grief, grieve
  ie – page 107

grievous
!! does not rhyme with
previous
gruesome
guarantee
★ related word *warranty*
may help you remember the
u, but note the single *r* in
guarantee and two *r*'s in
warranty
guard, guardian
related words *ward* and
warden may help you
remember the *u*
gullible
ible – page 174
gymnastics
'Greek *y*'
haemorrhage
haemo – page 221;
rrh – page 226
handicapped, handicapping
pp – page 154
handkerchief
★ used by *hand*
harass, harassed
★ we're quite busy but
hardly harassed
heinous
ei – page 107
hereditary
ary – page 190 (the *a* is
often slurred in speech)
hideous
eous – page 197
hierarchy
ie – page 107

holistic
!! not 'whole'
honorary, honourable
★ related to *honorarium*;
or, our – page 202
hygiene, hygienic
y = 'Greek /i/';
ie – page 107
hymn
y = 'Greek /i/';
★ for the *n*, think of *hymnal*
hypochondria,
hypochondriac
y = 'Greek /i/';
ch = 'Greek /k/';
hypo – page 222
hypocrisy, hypocrite
'Greek /i/';
hypo – page 222
isy – page 180
hysteria, hysterically
y = 'Greek /i/';
hysterical + *-ly*
idiosyncrasy
y = 'Greek /i/';
asy – page 180

---

il-, im- in-, ir-
*il*legal, *il*legible, *il*legitimate,
*il*literate, *il*logical, *im*moral,
*im*mortal, *in*accurate, *ir*regular,
*ir*relevant, *ir*resistible,
*ir*responsible
  The structure of all these words
is clearly *il - legal, im - moral,
in - accurate, ir - regular,* and so
on, so the spelling should be
clear; see page 130.

imitate

immediate, immediately
 mm – page 159

immense
 mm – page 159;
 se – page 125

immigrant, immigration
 mm – page 158 (★ think of
 in - migrant)

imminent
 mm – page 159;
 ent – page 186

immune
 mm – page 159

implement

impostor
 or – page 192

improvise, improvisation
 ise – page 198

incidentally
 = *incidental - ly*

independence, independent
 en – page 181

infallible
 ible – page 174

infinite
 ★ related word *finite*

inflammable, inflammation
 able – page 174

innocence, innocent
 nn – page 159;
 en –page 181

inseparable
 ★ if you go back to its
 Latin origins, *separate*
 is related to the verb
 prepare

install, instalment
 ll, l – page 138

instil, instill
 both correct, but one *l* is
 commoner – page 138

integral
 !! not *intreg-*; related to
 integrate

interest, interesting

interrogate, interrogation
 rr – page 222

interrupt, interruption
 rr – page 222

irascible
 ★ related to *irate*;
 sc – page 220 at *esc*;
 ible – page 174

irritate, irritation, irritable
 rr – page 159;
 able – page 174

itinerary

jeopardy
 ★ see *leopard* below

jeweller, jewellery
 ll – page 153;
 ery – page 187

kidnapped, kidnapping,
 kidnapper
 pp – page 154

kilometre
 metre – page 83

knowledge, knowledgeable
 ★ related to *know*;
 dge – page 166;
 eable – page 176

laboratory
 ory – page 190

labyrinth
y = 'Greek /i/';
lacquer
laid
ai – page 120
language
u before *a*, just as it sounds
legitimate
ate – page 180
leisure
ei – page 107
length
★ related to *long*
leopard
★ think of a *leopard* in a
leotard being in *jeopardy*
liable
liaise, liaison
library
★ related word *librarian*
licence (*noun*), **license** (verb)
ce, se – page 125
lieutenant
★ the original idea is of
someone who can act *in lieu
of* someone else; the spelling
is French
liquefy
efy – page 195
literature
★ related to *literate,
literary*
longitude
!! not -*tit*-
luggage
gg – page 149
magnanimous

maintenance
ance – page 181
manageable
ea – page 176
manoeuvre
a French word with French
spelling; also in *hors
d'oeuvres*
margarine
marmalade
maroon
marriage
= *marry* + word-ending *age*
martyr
y = 'Greek /i/';
marvel, marvellous
ll – page 153
mayonnaise
mediaeval, medieval
both correct – page 97
medicine
★ related word *medical*
melancholy
ch = 'Greek /k/'
messenger
meteorology, meteorologist
★ related to *meteor*
mileage, milage
both correct
millennium
★ related to *million* and
annual
millionaire, millionairess
miniature
minuscule
!! related to *minus*; not
mini

mis**c**ellaneous
mis**ch**ie**f**, mischie**v**ous
  ie – page 107;
  !! *mischievous* does not
  rhyme with *previous*

mis-
  misshapen, misspelt, misspent =
  mis - shapen, mis - spelt,
  mis - spent

mo**cc**asin
  ★ *moccasins* are *clearly*
  casual shoes
mo**d**e**r**n
  !! not *-dren*
mor**t**gage
  ★ related to *mortality*
mo**u**stache
  ★ think of the whiskers on a
  mouse
  ch = 'French /sh/'
mus**c**le
  ★ related word *muscular*
m**y**stery, mysterious, mystify
  y = 'Greek /i/', found in the
  'myths and mysteries' group
  of words – page 109
ne**c**e**ss**ary, necessity
  ★ the *cess* is related to *access*
  and *success*
negli**g**ence, negligent,
  negli**g**ible
  en – page 181;
  ible – page 174
ni**e**ce
  ie – page 107

ni**n**th
noti**c**eable
  ea – page 176
nu**c**lear
  !! some people pronounce
  this word /'njoohkjoolər/;
  ★ related to *nucleus*
n**u**isance
  an – page 181
ob**s**cene, obscenity
o**cc**asion, occasional
  cc – page 163
o**cc**upy, occupation
  cc – page 163
o**cc**ur, occurred, occurrence
  cc – page 163;
  rr – page 150;
  en – page 181
o**ff**ence, offensive
  ff – page 163;
  ce, se – page 125
o**ff**er, offered, offering
  ff – page 163;
  r – page 150
o**m**it, omission, omi**tt**ed
  m – page 163;
  tt – page 150
o**pp**onent
  pp – page 163;
  ent – page 186
o**pp**ortunity
  pp – page 163
o**pp**osite, opposition
  pp – page 163
ord**i**nary, ordinarily
o**u**trageous
  eous – page 197

p*a*id
 ai – page 120
pam*ph*let
 ph = 'Greek /f/'
para*ff*in
 so called because of its
 lack of *affinity* to other
 chemicals
para*l*lel, paralle*l*ed,
 parallelogram
 l – page 154
para*l*ysis, paral*y*se, paralytic
 lysis – page 223
 yse – page 200
parl*i*ament, parliamentary
pas*s*enger
pastime
peac*e*able
 ea – page 176
perman*e*nt
 ent – page 186
persever*a*nce
 ance – page 181
persist*e*nce, persistent
 en – page 181
p*h*enom*e*non
plaus*i*ble
 ible – page 174
play*wright*
 !! nothing to do with
 writing;
 ★ *wright* is related to
 wrought, as also in
 shipwright and *cartwright*
pleasant
 ★ related to *please*;
 an – page 186

pos*s*ess, possession,
 possessive
pos*s*ible possibility, possibly
 ible – page 174
post*h*umous
practic*ally*
 = *practical - ly*
practi*c*e (noun), practi*s*e
 (verb)
 ce, se – page 126
pre*c*ede, preceding
 cede – page 218
prede*c*essor
 ★ *cess* as in *success*;
 or – page 192
pre*f*er, pre*f*erred, pre*f*erable,
 preference
 f – page 164;
 rr – page 150;
 able – page 174;
 en – page 181
pre*p*aration
 ★ related word *prepare*
prevalent
 en – page 186
privil*e*ge
 ege – page 135;
 ★ related word *legal*
prob*a*ble, probably
 able – page 174;
pro*c*eed, proceedings,
 pro*c*edure
 ceed – page 218;
 !! note *procedure*
pro*f*ess, profession, profes*s*or
 ★ related word *confess*;
 or – page 193

profit, profited
t – page 150
pronunciation
!! said and written as *nun*
prophecy (noun), prophesy
(verb)
c, s – page 126
psychiatry, psychology,
psychiatrist, psychologist,
etc
psych – page 225
publicly
ly – page 202
pursue, pursuit
pyjamas
pyramid
y = 'Greek /i/'
quay
a French word, with French
spelling
questionnaire
note nn
queue, queued, queuing
raspberry
★ raspberries often
shortened to rasps
really
= real - ly
rebellion, rebellious
ll – page 153
recede
cede – page 218
receive, receipt
ei – page 107
recognize, recognise
★ related to cognition;
ize, ise – page 198

recommend, recommendation
c, mm – page 162
reconnaissance
a French word
recruit
recur, recurring, recurrence
c – page 164;
rr – page 150;
ence – page 181
redundant, redundancy
an – page 181;
cy – page 126
refer, referee, reference,
referred, referral
f – page 164;
en – page 181;
r, rr – page 150
refrigerator
but fridge
regrettable
tt – page 150;
able – page 174
relief, relieve
ie – page 107
remember, remembrance
br – page 104;
ance – page 181
reminiscence, reminiscent
sc – see esc, page 220;
en – page 181
remit, remittance
tt – page 150;
ance – page 181
repetition, repetitive
★ the pronunciations of the
two words together show
the correct spelling -petit-

repri*e*ve
 ie – page 107
require
 q – page 164
resemble, resemblance
 ance – page 181
reservoir
 ★ a *reservoir reserves*
 water;
 the *oir* is a French spelling,
 as also in *boudoir* and
 memoir
resign
 ★ related word *resignation*
resistance, resistant
 an – page 181
responsible, responsibility
 ible – page 174
restaurant
 but *restaurateur*
resurrect, resurrection
resuscitate
reversible
 ible – page 174
rheumatism
 rh = 'Greek /r/'
rhyme, rhythm
 rh = 'Greek /r/';
 y = 'Greek /i/'
sacrifice, sacrificial
sacrilege, sacrilegious
 ege – page 135;
 ★ related to *legal*
said
 ai – page 120
sandwich
sapphire

satisfactory
 ory – page 191
scavenge, scavenger
schedule
 ch = 'Greek /k/'
scheme
 ch = 'Greek /k/'
scissors
 sc – page 24
scurrilous
secondary
 ary – page 190
secretary
 ary – page 189;
 ★ related to *secretarial*
sensible
 ible – page 174
separate, separation
 ★ if you go back to its Latin
 origins, *separate* is related to
 the verb *prepare*
sergeant
several
severely
 = *severe* - *ly*
shepherd
 ★ a 'sheep *herd*'
sheriff
 ff – page 132
sieve
 ie – page 107
similar, similarity,
 similarly
simultaneous
 eous – page 197
sincerely
 = *sincere* - *ly*

skil**f**ul
l – page 139
*somer*sault
sover*eign*, sovereignty
spa*g*he*tti*
specific*ally*
ally – page 202
stea*d*fast
!! *stedfast* only in the
motto of the Boys'
Brigade
strength
★ related to *strong*
su**b**tle, subtlety, subtly
suc*cc*ess, successful,
success**o**r
cc – page 163;
or – page 193
su**ff**icient
ff – page 163;
ent – page 184
suggest, suggestion
gg – page 163
super*cil*ious
superintend**e**nt
ent – page 186
super*sede*
sede – page 218
super*vise*, supervi**so**r
ise – page 198;
or – page 192
su**pp**ose, supposing,
supposedly
pp – page 163
surp*rise*, surprised,
surprising
ise – page 198

su**rr**ound
survi**vo**r
or – page 193

syl-, sym-, syn-, sys-
*syl*lable, *syl*labus, *sy*mbol,
*sy*mbolic, *sy*mmetrical, *sy*mpathy,
*sy*mpathetic, *sy*mpathize,
*sy*mphony, *sy*nagogue, *sy*nthesis,
*sy*nthetic, *sy*stem, *sy*stematic:
all these have the 'Greek /i/' *y*;
for the double letters, see
page 160.

*sy*ringe
y = 'Greek /i/'
*sy*ru*p*
target**e**d, targeting
t – page 150
tari**ff**
ff – page 132
temp**e**rament,
temperamental
★ related to *temper*
temp**e**rature
★ related to *temper*
temp**o**rary, temporarily
ary – page 190
tendency
ency – page 186
te**rr**ace, territory
★ related to Latin *terra*
'land';
ory – page 191
te**rr**ible, terrific,
terrified
★ related word *terror*

thief, thieves
 ie – page 107
threshold
tobacco, tobacconist
tomorrow
 !! one *m*, as in *morning*
tonsillitis
 ll – page 154;
 itis – page 222
traffic, trafficking
 ff – page 132;
 ck – page 151
tranquil, tranquillity
 l, ll – page 154
**transferred, transferable,
 transference**
 rr, r – page 152;
 able – page 174;
 ence – page 185
treachery, treacherous
 ★ related word *treason*;
 ery – page 189
true, truly
 loss of *e* – page 104
turquoise
twelfth
 ★ related to *twelve*
tyranny, tyrannical
 y = 'Greek /i/';
 ★ related word *tyrant*
underrated
 = *under - rated*
unduly
 see *duly*
unforgettable
 tt – page 150;
 able – page 174

unforgivable
 able – page 174
unnatural
 = *un - natural*
unnecessary
 = *un - necessary*
until
 but *till*
usually
 = *usual - ly*
vaccine, vaccinate
vacuum
valuable
 loss of *e* – page 99
vanguard
 ★ from *guard*
vegetable
 ★ related word *vegetation*
vehicle
 ★ related word *vehicular*
vengeance
 ea – page 100
veterinary, veterinarian
vigilance, vigilant
 ★ related word *vigilante*
visitor
 or – page 193
weird
 ei – page 107
wholly
 ll – page 104
wield
 ie – page 107
withhold
 = *with - hold*
woollen, woolly
 ll – page 153

worshi**pp**ed, worshi**pp**er
pp – page 154
yie**ld**
ie – page 107

yogurt, **y**og**h**urt, **y**og**hou**rt
all correct
zoology
zoo – page 227

4
One word or two?

Among the spelling errors that many people make is writing what should be a single word as two separate words, or on the other hand writing what should be two words as a single word.

While some of these mistakes may be no more than slips of the pen, others may arise from confusion over which spellings represent which meanings.

This chapter tackles the most common examples of confusion about whether to write one word or two.

all
Most compound words beginning with 'all' are spelt with **all** in full, usually followed by a hyphen:

all-embracing, all-knowing, all-out, all-powerful, all-purpose, all-rounder, allspice, all-star, all-time, all-weather, etc

A few **all** compounds may be confused with words beginning with **al-**. See the entries below.

almighty, all mighty

Write the adjective **almighty** as one word with one *l*:

Almighty God
There was an almighty row about the state of the pitch.

Do not confuse **almighty** with **all mighty** as two separate words:

They were all mighty warriors. (= All of them were mighty warriors)

almost, all most

Almost means 'nearly':

It was almost midnight when we reached the cottage.

Do not confuse **almost** with **all most** as two separate words:

People were rushing here and there, carrying boxes and files and piles of books. It was all most confusing. (= Everything was very confusing)

a lot

Always write this as two words:

✗ *This man has done alot for charity.*
✓ *This man has done a lot for charity.*

already, all ready

Already means 'before now' or 'before then':

The game had already started by the time we got there.

Do not confuse **already** with **all ready** as two separate words:

Are you all ready? (= Are all of you ready?)

all right

No matter what the meaning, this should be written as two words:

Were my answers all right? (= Were all my answers right?)
Are you all right? (= Are you okay?)

In the sense of 'okay', many people now write **alright**:

That's alright with me.

The spelling **alright** first appeared at the end of the 19th century and has become increasingly common through the 20th century and into the 21st. It could be argued that it would be logical to distinguish between **alright** and **all right** in the same way as English already distinguishes **altogether** and **all together** or **already** and **all ready**, but language is not always logical. Whatever its merits, **alright** has not yet gained acceptance as a correct spelling.

also, all so

Also means 'as well':

He was not just a landowner and a businessman. He was also an important historian and antiquary.

Do not confuse **also** with **all so** as two separate words:

I didn't see who hit me. It was all so sudden. (= The whole episode happened so suddenly)

although
Always write this as one word with one *l*:

Although I didn't know it at the time, I was talking to the girl who was one day to become my wife.

altogether, all together
Altogether means 'completely', 'in total', 'taking everything into account':

I think the government should scrap this law altogether.
It's been a very good day. Altogether I think we must have made about £800.
I've had a sleep and something to eat and altogether I'm feeling a lot better now.

All together means 'everyone at the same time or in the same place':

All together now. Sing up.
I've never seen so many guitarists all together on one stage.

always, all ways
Always means 'at all times':

He's always late.

All ways means 'every way':

I get more money in this job but shorter holidays. I suppose I can't have it all ways.

any more, anymore
The spelling in British English is always as two words:

We don't go there any more.

Anymore is correct only in American English:

They don't make small homes anymore.

anyone, any one
Anyone means 'any person at all':

If you see anyone coming, whistle.

★ As a spelling hint, notice that **anyone** could be replaced by **anybody**:

If you see anybody coming, whistle.

Any one means 'any individual one (person or thing)':

Use no more than half a pint of cream for any one of the puddings.

Any one will often be followed by a noun:

No more than one permit will be issued to any one person in any one hunting season.

anything
The normal spelling is as a single word:

Do you know anything about computers?

any way, anyway
Any way means 'any possible way or method':

We are here to help people in any way we can.

Anyway means 'in any case':

Anyway, it's time I was leaving.
It doesn't matter. I didn't want to go with them anyway.

as well
Always written as two words:

He's disappeared as well.

a while, awhile
The normal spelling in British English is as two words:

Let's just sit here for a while.
You may have to wait a while.
You could offer to wash the dishes just once in a while.

The spelling **awhile**, as one word, is found only in literature:

Stay yet awhile! speak to me once again; . . .

Percy Bysshe Shelley, *Adonais*

Awhile is not used in everyday contexts in British English, and even in poetry there is no particular need to use this literary form. Note also that it is not correct to use **awhile** after a preposition (such as *for* or *in*). Since it is never incorrect to write **a while**, but sometimes incorrect to write **awhile**, it is safer to use **a while** in all circumstances.

In American English, on the other hand, **awhile** is commonly used in everyday contexts, even after a preposition:

A common complaint among people who've lived in Reno awhile is that it's become too much like everyplace else.
After awhile, he pulled into a parking lot.

cannot, can not
The normal spelling is as a single word, **cannot**:

I cannot imagine what he was doing there.
Science cannot yet provide the answers to all our questions.

You only write **can not** as two separate words when the *not* is closely linked to what follows it in the sentence, as for example in the linked phrases *not only . . . but also . . .*:

Minimizing the amount of rubbish you throw away can not only protect natural resources but also save you money.

daresay, dare say
Both **daresay** and **dare say** are correct:

I daresay she might win a medal in the Olympics.
I dare say I could learn Japanese if I wanted to.

ever, -ever
When **ever** is used to emphasize question words such as *how*, *why* or *where*, it is written as a separate word:

Where ever did you get that idea from?
Why ever does she wear such strange clothes?
What ever shall we do now?
How ever did people manage without mobile phones?

When **ever** means 'any — at all' or 'no matter which —', it is attached to the word it modifies:

With her blond hair, upturned nose and tight black dresses, Holly is a sensation wherever she goes.
Whatever he does, he does to the best of his ability.

Take whichever book you want.
She is my baby and I'll carry her however I please.

See also *forever, for ever* below.

every day, everyday
Every day means 'on all days':

I visit my mother every day.

Everyday means 'occurring on all days', 'normal', 'not special':

Bombs are an everyday occurrence here.
Our sofa-beds are designed for everyday use, either as a sofa or as a bed.
Have you ever wondered where some of the expressions we use in everyday language come from?

everyone, every one
Everyone means 'every single person':

Everyone thought I was crazy, but I didn't care.
I have the same feelings about this as everyone else.

★ **Everyone** can be replaced by **everybody**:

I have the same feelings about this as everybody else.

Every one means 'each individual one' or 'every single one':

I dropped the pile of plates I was carrying and every one of them broke.
The hotel has been designed so that every one of its rooms has a view of the Taj Mahal.

everything
The normal spelling is as one word:

I can carry everything I might need in this bag.
This book tells you everything you need to know about your cat.

forever, for ever
The spelling **forever** is correct in all senses of the word:

Would you like to live forever?
It took forever to fill out all the forms.
He's forever losing his umbrella.
Ayr United forever!

In the sense of 'for all future time', the spelling **for ever** as two words is also correct:

Our oil supplies won't last for ever.

Some authorities, but not all, allow the two-word spelling also for the meaning 'a very long time':

The police seemed to take for ever to arrive.

The two-word spelling is not used in American English.
   In the phrase **for ever and ever, for ever** and **forever** are both considered correct and are equally common:

Will the universe last for ever and ever?
We'll be married forever and ever.

Both **forever more** and **for evermore** are correct in British English, and are equally common:

I will love you forever more.
He wanted his name to live on for evermore.

The spelling **forevermore** as one word is correct only in American English:

I wish I could live forevermore.

-ful, full

The suffix -**ful** is added to a word for a container to indicate the amount held by the container:

bagful, basketful, cupful, handful, jugful, mouthful, plateful, sackful, spoonful, etc

It must be understood that words ending in -**ful** denote quantities that the containers could or would hold, and do not imply that the substance or material referred to is actually in the container: for example, a *spoonful* of sugar is still a spoonful once it has been stirred into a cup of coffee, and a *cupful* of sugar is still a cupful when it has been mixed with other ingredients to make a cake.

Note that the plural of *bagful, cupful, spoonful,* etc is *bagfuls, cupfuls, spoonfuls,* etc.

On the other hand, phrases such as *three bags full of rubbish* or *two cups full of water* are referring to the *containers* (bags or cups) rather than to quantities. Note the difference, then, between the following two sentences:

I put three bagfuls of rubbish into the dustbin. ('three bagfuls' denotes the quantity of rubbish; the bags themselves may not have been put into the dustbin)
I put three bags full of rubbish into the dustbin. (This means that I actually put three bags into the dustbin, and all three were full of rubbish.)

Similarly:

He drank a whole jugful of lemonade.
She brought a jug full of lemonade.

In accordance with the above explanation, the spelling **brim-full** (= full to the brim) should be preferred to *brimful*, but in fact **brimful** is by far the commoner form:

The book is brim-full of information about vampires.
He was brimful of bright ideas.

Chock-full, however, is always spelt with two *l*'s:

The whole room was chock-full of books.

inasmuch as, in as much as
Both are correct, but the first form is found slightly more often than the second:

Norway and Turkey were literally in the front line against the former Soviet Union during the Cold War inasmuch as they shared a boundary with it.
Our imagination is like our muscles in as much as its ability can be increased by exercise.

in case
This is always written as two words:

What to do in case of fire: ring the fire alarm and leave the building immediately by the nearest exit.

in fact
Always written as two words:

It's Sunday morning and it's still raining. Pouring, in fact.

insofar as, in so far as
Both are correct, but the second form is slightly commoner than the first:

Attention is also given to history, the social sciences and politics, insofar as these impact on culture.
In so far as the cancer of society is greed, the cure must include generosity.

in spite of
In spite is always written as two words:

In spite of her youth, she was regarded as an important artist.

instead
Instead is always written as one word:

Why don't you go for a walk instead of watching television?
Don't go and see the film. Read the book instead.

into, in to
Into is a preposition used to indicate movement from outside to inside something, movement against something, or change from one state to another:

Suddenly, armed men burst into the room and began firing.
Tuck your shirt into your trousers.
After a stunned silence, they all broke into wild applause.
The boy slowly backed away until he bumped into a tree.
In this story, a prince turns into a frog and falls in love with a frog princess.
Several of his books were translated into Latin in the early 12th century.

Two informal new senses of **into** are 'keen on' and 'involved with':

I'm more into jazz than rap.
She's got into drugs and booze and she looks ill.

In to consists of a preposition **in** (meaning 'into a place') and the preposition **to** (sometimes followed by a verb). The two words should therefore be written separately whenever the meaning of the sentence shows that the **in** and the **to** are not acting together to express any of the meanings given in the examples above:

The midwife came in to say the baby had arrived.
When the bell went, we all went in to dinner.
Listen in to our opera highlights tonight at seven o'clock.
The news came in to us while I was in bed.
Keep your elbows tucked in to your sides. (= tucked in close to your sides)

Sometimes it really does not matter whether you write **into** or **in to**:

We tucked into a hearty breakfast.
We tucked in to a hearty breakfast.

In cases like this, listen to how you say the sentence and write what you say.

maybe, may be
Maybe means 'perhaps'. It is always written as one word:

Maybe she'll come, and maybe she won't.
Maybe he'll never find what he's looking for in life.

May be is a phrase comprising the verb **may** and the verb **be**. The sentence construction with **may be** is therefore different from that with **maybe**. Compare the following sentences:

It may be that he'll never find what he's looking for.
Maybe he'll never find what he's looking for.

methinks

This archaic word, meaning 'it seems to me', is still often used humorously. Often those who use it spell it as two words, but it should always be written as a single word:

Methinks it's time to move on.

no one, no-one

In principle, the same distinction should be made between **no-one** and **no one** as is made between **anyone** and **any one**, **everyone** and **every one**, **someone** and **some one**. **No-one** means 'nobody', just as **anyone** means 'anybody', **everyone** means 'everybody' and **someone** means 'somebody':

anybody	*anyone*
everybody	*everyone*
nobody	*no-one* (with a hyphen added to separate the two *o*'s)
somebody	*someone*

Unfortunately, language is not always logical, and the most common spelling nowadays is not **no-one** but **no one**, although **no-one** is also perfectly correct (and is definitely preferable):

No one complained at the time.
There was no one there.
I told you what might happen but no-one ever listens to me.

Do not write **✗noone** as a single word:

✗ *There's noone here but me.*

No one also means 'no single individual (person or thing)':

No one person could take on all those jobs.
They believe that no one religion holds all the truths.
No one book could tell you all you need to know.

of course
Always written as two words:

Of course you can go if you want to.
Of course, things were different when I was your age.

onto, on to
Unlike **into**, which is a well-established word that has to be used in certain contexts, **onto** is not yet accepted by everyone as a correct form. It is therefore never wrong to write **on to** as two separate words:

The coin fell on to the floor.
Let's move on to the next question.
Hold on to the rope.

However, many people now use **onto** in the sense of 'to a position on something':

The coin fell onto the floor.
Pipe the remaining icing onto the cake to make a floral design.

Although not acceptable to everyone, this usage is so well established that it must now be considered correct.

per cent, percent

In British English **per cent** is usually written as two words:

Fifty per cent of the population of Ghana are Christian and 13 per cent are Muslim.

In American English, it is usually written as one word:

The richest 20 percent of the world's population eat eleven times as much meat and seven times as much fish as the poorest 20 percent.

sometime, some time

Sometime means 'at some point in time':

I am well into my next novel and hope to finish it sometime early next year.
I'd love to go to the Lake District sometime.

Some time means 'a little time':

I'd like to spend some time in the Lake District this summer.

Similarly, **sometimes** means 'occasionally', 'from time to time':

Sometimes I just feel like screaming.
These apparitions attracted large crowds, sometimes as many as 20,000 people.

Some times means 'certain times', 'a number of times'. It usually follows a preposition (such as *at*):

It is quite normal for your blood pressure to be higher at some times than at others.
At some times of the year, the Earth is much hotter than at other times.

straight away, straightaway

Both are correct, but the spelling as two words is the commoner of the two:

Farmers should get their applications in straight away.
If you cannot get the information we need straightaway, do not worry.

straightforward

In the sense of 'simple', 'obvious' or 'uncomplicated', always written as one word:

The solution to the problem is pretty straightforward.

thank you

This is normally written as two words:

Thank you all for your support.

After the verb *say*, **thank you** may optionally be placed in quotation marks, or it may be hyphenated:

I just wanted to say thank you to you for arranging our stay in London.
I would just like to say 'thank you' to all of you for your support.
We just want to say thank-you for these lovely gifts.

As a noun, or before a noun, **thank you** should be hyphenated:

A big thank-you to everyone who helped make the fete a success.
Have you written your thank-you letters yet?

worthwhile, worth while

Before a noun, write **worthwhile** as a single word:

It should be a great concert and it's in aid of a very worthwhile cause.

After a verb, both **worthwhile** and **worth while** are correct:

I decided it wasn't worthwhile checking every calculation again.
It's just not worth while to repair an old CD player.

5
Words that are often confused

There are three categories of word included in this chapter:

1. Words that sound the same, or very similar, and which are therefore sometimes confused, e.g. *birth* and *berth*, or *mystic* and *mystique*.

2. Words, such as *bell* and *belle*, one of which causes no spelling problems at all while the other is often misspelt.

3. Words that are unalike in sound but similar enough in spelling for them frequently to be confused by slips of the pen (or slips of the brain): for example *dairy* and *diary*, *prostate* and *prostrate*, *quiet* and *quite*.

> **NOTE**
> Not all possible meanings or uses of the words are
> given below, only sufficient to clearly distinguish the
> spellings. In some cases, the words are distinguished
> by part-of-speech labels such as noun and verb.

accede = to agree to;
accede to (the throne)

exceed = to be greater than

accept = to take; to believe,
agree to

except (*preposition*) = not
including; (*verb*) = to
exclude: *present company
excepted*

access = use of, contact
with; a sudden fit: *an access
of generosity*

excess = too much;
excesses = outrageous acts:
excesses of the previous regime

adapter = person who
adapts (a play, etc)

adaptor = fitting into which
an electric plug is inserted

addition = something added

edition = copies of a book,
magazine etc printed at one
time

adverse = unfavourable

averse = not liking
something

advice (*noun*)

advise (*verb*) = to give advice

affect (*verb*) = to cause a
change, influence

effect (*noun*) = result, consequence; (*verb*) = to cause,
bring about

aid = help

aide = assistant, adviser

ail = to trouble or cause
pain to

ale = beer

aisle = passageway

isle = island

allay = to lessen (fear, hunger, etc)

alley = narrow street or passage-way

ally = political or military associate

allude = to refer to

elude = to escape from

allusion = reference to something

illusion = false impression

altar = place of worship

alter = to change

amend = to correct or improve

emend = to correct errors in (a text)

angel = heavenly being

angle = corner

annex = to take possession of territory

annexe or **annex** = additional building

arc = curved line (★ *c* as in *arch*)

ark = boat for animals

artist = painter, sculptor, etc; skilful person

artiste or **artist** = theatrical or circus performer

ascent = climbing

assent = agreement

augur = soothsayer; augur well/ill

auger = pointed tool

aural = relating to the ear or listening

oral = relating to the mouth or speech

bail = money paid for release of prisoner; part of wicket;
  bail out = to help someone in difficulty

bale = bundle of hay;
  bale out or **bail out** = to get rid of water from a boat; to parachute from an aircraft

baited = having bait to attract prey

bated as in *with bated breath*

ballet = dance

ballot = vote (★ *ballot* and *vote*)

balmy = warm, pleasant

barmy = crazy

bare = naked

bear (*noun*) = animal; (*verb*) = to carry, support

base (*noun*) = bottom part; headquarters; (*verb*) = to use as a basis

bass = deep male singing voice;
   double bass = large stringed instrument

baton = stick for conductor or runner (★ a *baton* for a *conductor*)

batten (*noun*) = piece of wood; (*verb*) = to fasten down (★ *batten* and *fasten*)

bazaar = market (★ a *bazaar* is a *market*)

bizarre = odd

beach = sand beside sea (★ a *beach* is near the *sea*)

beech = tree (★ a *beech* tree)

bean = vegetable

been = part of verb *be*

beat (*verb*) = to hit; to do better than; (*noun*) = route patrolled by police officer

beet = vegetable

beer = drink

bier = support for coffin

bell = thing that rings

belle = beautiful girl: *the belle of the ball*

berry = fruit   **beret** = cap   **bury** = to put into ground and cover

berth = bed or cabin on ship; place for ship at quay

birth = being born

bite = to cut with teeth   **bight** = curve in coastline   **byte** = unit of computer memory

block (*noun*) = lump; block-age; (*verb*) = to cause a blockage

bloc = group of countries

blond = referring to male person

blonde = referring to female person: *She's gone blonde*; also **blond** if referring directly to hair: *She has blonde (or blond) hair*

boar = male pig, wild pig

bore = dull, uninteresting person; nuisance

boor = rude person

bogey = golf score; evil spirit; dry nasal mucus

bogie = low truck, part of railway engine

bogy = **bogey** or **bogie**

born = coming into the world: *born on New Year's Day*; caused by: *anger born of fear*

borne = having given birth to: *She had borne six children*; carried, tolerated: *a long illness, bravely borne*

bough = branch of tree

bow = front of boat; act of bending one's body politely

boy = male child

buoy = marker to guide shipping;
  buoy up = to elate

brake = device for stopping vehicle;
  shooting brake = type of car

break = to come to pieces, to fail to observe (a rule or law), and other senses

brassiere = item of clothing

brazier = holder for burning coal

breach = break, act of breaking through (★ *breach* and *break*)

breech = part of gun;
breeches = trousers

breath = air breathed

breathe = to take in air

bridal = of a bride

bridle (*noun*) = horse's harness; (*verb*) = to react angrily

broach = to open (a barrel), mention (a subject)

brooch = piece of jewellery

but = on the other hand

butt (*noun*) = end of cigarette; object of ridicule; barrel; (*verb*) = to hit with head or horns

buy = to pay money for

by = beside, etc

bye = short for *goodbye*; run scored in cricket

caddie or **caddy** (in golf)

caddy = box for tea

callous = cruel, unfeeling

callus = hard skin

cannon = gun;
 cannon into = to collide with

canon = clergyman; musical composition; set of principles; authoritative books

canvas = material

canvass (in elections)

carat = unit of weight for precious stones; standard of purity of gold

caret = mark to show that something is missing

carrot = vegetable

cash = money

cache = secret store

cast (*noun*) = actors; appearance; mould; (*verb*) = to throw; to make

caste = social class

caster or **castor** = sugar sprinkler;
 caster sugar or **castor sugar**

castor = wheel on chair; **castor oil**

causal = causing

casual = informal

ceiling = upper surface of room; limit

sealing = act of closing with a seal

cell (in prison, in body, etc); group

sell = to give for money

censor = official who rates acceptability of films, books, etc

censure = blame, reprimand

cent = money, coin

sent = past tense of *send*

scent (*noun*) = perfume; (*verb*) = to smell; to have an inkling

cereal = corn, etc (★ *Ceres* was the Roman goddess of agriculture)

serial = series of programmes (★ *series* and *serial*)

cheap = not expensive

cheep = sound made by small bird

check = to make sure about something; to put a stop to

cheque = slip of paper ordering payment of money

chilly = cold

chilli = pepper

choir = singers (★ *church choirs chant*)

quire = quantity of paper (★ *quire* = a *quantity*)

choose = /chooz/ (present tense)

chose = /chohz/ (past tense)

chord = musical notes played together; line joining points on a circle

cord = string; flex; ribbed fabric;
   umbilical cord, spinal cord, vocal cords

chute = channel for sliding down; parachute

shoot (*verb*) = to fire a gun; to move quickly; (*noun*) = stem of plant

cite = to quote; to summon to a law court

site = place

sight = power of seeing; something seen

cloth = material, fabric

clothe = to put clothes on

coarse = rough, rude

course (*noun*) = series; lessons; route; (*verb*) = to run, flow;
 of course

cocoa = substance like chocolate

cacao = source of cocoa and chocolate

college = place of study

collage = form of art

comma = punctuation mark

coma = unconsciousness

compare = to look at differences and similarities

compere = host of show

complacent = self-satisfied

complaisant = happy to comply

compliment = praise

complement (*noun*) = something that goes well with something else; complete amount, group, crew, etc; (*verb*) = to go well with; to make complete

complimentary = praising, flattering; supplied free: *a complimentary ticket*

complementary = going well together; forming a whole; supplying what each other lacks

concert = musical performance;
 concerted effort; in
concert = working together

consort (*noun*) = husband or wife of monarch; group of musicians;
 in consort = working together;
 consort with = to be regularly in the company of

confident = self-assured; convinced

confidant (masculine) and **confidante** (feminine) = person in whom you confide

corps = group of people

corpse = dead body

correspondent = letter-writer; reporter

co-respondent = person cited in divorce case

council = body of officials

counsel (*noun*) = advice; courtroom lawyer; (*verb*) = to advise

councillor = member of council

counsellor = adviser (a member of an advice-giving *council* may be called a *counsellor*: the Marriage Guidance *Council* has marriage-guidance *counsellors* and the Privy *Council* has Privy *Counsellors* or Privy *Councillors*)

courtesy = politeness

curtsy = respectful gesture performed by women

creak = squeaky noise

creek = inlet, water channel

crevasse = deep crack in ice

crevice = narrow crack

crochet /'krohshay/ = craft like knitting

crotchet /'krochit/ = musical note

curb = to restrict or restrain

kerb = edge of pavement

currant = small dried grape or berry

current (*noun*) = flow of water, air or electricity; (*adjective*) = of the present time

cygnet = young swan

signet = type of ring

damn (*noun*) = swear word; (*verb*) = to condemn

dam = barrier across water; female animal

dear = loved; expensive

deer = animal

decent = respectable

descent = going down

defuse = to remove the fuse from; to remove tension from

diffuse (*verb*) = to spread widely; (*adjective*) = scattered, spread widely

dependant (*noun*) = person who depends on someone financially

dependent (*adjective*) = depending on

desert (*noun*) = hot dry place; (*verb*) = to leave

dessert = sweet course of meal

device = tool or contrivance

devise = to plan or invent

dew = moisture

due = liable, appropriate, expected

diary = book

dairy = place where milk, cream, cheese, etc are processed or bought

die = to stop living (Note: *die, dying, dies, died*)

dye = colour (Note: *dye, dyeing, dyes, dyed*)

dingy = dull

dinghy = boat

disc = round flat object; spelling used especially in the recording industry;
  compact disc

disk round flat object; spelling used especially in the computer industry;
  floppy disk

discomfort = slight pain

discomfit = to embarrass or disconcert

discreet = tactful, cautious

discrete = separate (★ *discrete* and *separate* both end in *te*)

discuss = to talk about

discus = round flat object thrown in sport

diverse = varied, different

divers = several

doe = female deer

doh or **do** = musical note

dough = mixture of flour and water

dose (*noun*) = amount; (*verb*) = to give medicine to

doze = sleep

draft = rough version; order for payment by a bank

draught = current of air; act of drinking; minimum depth of water for ship; **draughts** = board game

dual = double

duel = fight

eerie = weird and frightening

eyrie = nest (★ *eyries* have *young* birds in them)

elicit = to get (information, etc)

illicit = unlawful

eligible = suitable, qualified

illegible = unreadable

emigrant = person who leaves native country

immigrant = person who comes into a country

eminent = distinguished, important

imminent = about to happen

---

enquire, enquiry, inquire, inquiry
Both *en-* and *in-* are correct. The verb can be spelt *enquire* or *inquire* with no distinction of meaning. As for the noun, *enquiry* is preferred by some people for a simple question and *inquiry* for an investigation: *the enquiry desk; a government inquiry*. But this is not a hard-and-fast rule.

---

ensure = to make sure

insure = to take out insurance

envelop = to cover, surround

envelope = cover for letter

exercise = activity for health and fitness

exorcise = to get rid of (a ghost)

exciting = thrilling

exiting = leaving

faint = almost too slight to be seen or heard

feint (*noun*) = misleading pretend attack; (*adjective*) = printed with faint lines

fair (*adjective*) = blond; just, appropriate; (*noun*) = place with amusements; place for selling

fare (*noun*) = payment for travel ticket; food; (*verb*) = to do well or badly

farther (used only with reference to distance)

further (*adjective*) = additional; (can also be used in reference to distance); (*verb*) = to help or advance

fate = unavoidable happening

fete or **fête** = outdoor festival

fawn (*noun*) = baby deer; colour; (*verb*) = to flatter

faun = mythical being

feat = achievement

feet = plural of *foot*

final (*adjective*) = last; (*noun*) = last match in competition

finale /fiˈnahli/ = final scene or event

flair = talent

flare = flash of light; flame

flee = to run away

flea = tiny insect

flu = influenza   **flue** = pipe for smoke or gas   **flew** = past tense of *fly*

flour = powder for baking

flower = coloured part of plant

flow = smooth movement

floe = sheet of floating ice

fool = stupid person

full = having no empty space

forebear or **forbear** = ancestor

forbear = to refrain from doing

forward = towards the front

foreword = preface

foul (*adjective*) = dirty, disgusting, offensive; (*noun*) = breaking of rule in sport

fowl = chicken, turkey or duck

frank = open, honest

franc = money, coin (★ the money of *France*)

freeze = to be very cold; to harden with cold

frieze = wall decoration

gamble = to bet money on cards, races, etc

gambol = to jump about

gaol = jail

goal = aim in life, place to aim at

gate = hinged barrier

gait = way of walking

gild = to cover with gold

guild = association

gilt = gold material

guilt = shame felt after doing wrong; fact of having done wrong

glacier = mass of moving ice

glazier = person who puts glass in windows

gorilla = ape

guerrilla or **guerilla** = member of fighting force

great = big; wonderful

grate (*noun*) = part of fireplace; (*verb*) = to rub or grind; to irritate

grill = part of cooker

grille or **grill** = framework of metal bars

grisly = horrifying   **grizzly** (as in *grizzly bear*)   **gristly** = full of gristle

hail (*noun*) = frozen rain; (*verb*) = to call to; **hail from** = to come from

hale = healthy: *hale and hearty*

hair = growth on head

hare = animal; **hare-brained; harelip**

hall = large room

haul (*verb*) = to pull; (*noun*) = stolen goods

hangar = aircraft shed

hanger (for clothes)

heal = to mend or cure

heel (on foot)

heart = centre; part of body

hart = male deer

heroine = female hero

heroin = drug

higher = more high

hire = to rent

hoar = frost

whore = prostitute

hoard = secret store

horde = crowd

hole = gap

whole = complete

horse = animal

hoarse = rough (of voice)

hue = colour; shouting; hue and cry

hew = to cut (wood)

human (*noun*) = person; (*adjective*) = of people

humane = compassionate

idle = lazy, not busy

idol = image worshipped

incite = to encourage

insight = wisdom, discernment (★ *sight* as in *seeing*)

ingenious = very clever

ingenuous = naïve, trusting

its = of it: *A snake sheds its skin every three months.*

it's = it is: *It's time to go*; = it has: *Look at that snake. It's got a frog in its mouth.*

jam = sticky food; blocked traffic

jamb = door frame

key = tool for opening door; musical scale; button on keyboard

quay = harbour

lane = narrow street or path

lain = past participle of *lay*

lair = animal's den

layer = covering or thickness spread over

lama = Buddhist monk

llama = animal

lea = meadow

lee = shelter

lead = metal

led = past tense of verb *lead*

leak = escape of liquid or gas

leek = vegetable

leant = past tense of *lean*

lent = past tense of *lend*

Lent = time before Easter

lesson = teaching

lessen = to become less

liar = person who tells lies

lyre = musical instrument

licence (*noun*)

license (*verb*)

lightning = flash of light that accompanies thunder

lightening = present participle of *lighten*

liquor = alcoholic drinks

liqueur = strong alcoholic drink

load = amount carried

lode = vein of metal ore

loan = lending; something lent

lone = alone

loathe = to hate

loath or **loth** = unwilling

local = nearby

locale /loh'kahl/ = place, locality

loose = not tight

lose = to cease to have

loot = things stolen

lute = musical instrument

lumber = unwanted goods

lumbar = of the back

madam = polite form of address to women

Madame = French equivalent of *Mrs*

made = past tense of *make*

maid = girl; servant

magnet = object that attracts metal

magnate = wealthy businessman

male = the sex that men and boys belong to

mail = post; armour

mane = hair on animal's neck

main = (*adjective*) chief; (*noun*) the ocean

manner = way

manor = country house

mare = female horse

mayor = elected head of town council

marshal (*noun*) = sheriff; (*verb*) = to arrange, assemble

martial = relating to war and soldiers

marten = animal

martin = bird

mat = rug

matt = not glossy

maze = puzzle

maize = corn

medal = award

meddle = to interfere

meat = beef, mutton, etc

meet (*verb*) = to get together; (*adjective*) = suitable

mete out = to impose (punishment)

metal = gold, silver, copper, etc

mettle = strength of character, courage: *be on one's mettle*

meter = measuring device

metre = unit of measurement; rhythm in poetry

mews = stable; housing

muse = spirit of poetry

might (*noun*) = strength; (*verb*: as in *I might come*)

mite = small animal, child, amount or coin

miner = mine-worker

minor (*noun*) = young person; (*adjective*) = lesser, unimportant

moan = to cry softly with grief or pain

mourn = to weep for loss of

moat = water round castle

mote = speck

moose = animal

mousse = foam

moral (*adjective*) = ethically good; (*noun*) principle learned from story;
morals = principles of good behaviour

morale /mə'rahl/ = state of confidence or contentment

motive = reason

motif = pattern or design; recurring theme

muscle = body tissue (★*muscular*)

mussel = shellfish

mystic = mysterious or miraculous, spiritual

mystique /mi'steek/ = mysterious element

naval = relating to the navy

navel = shallow hole in abdomen; **navel orange**

nave = part of church

knave = bad person; playing card

need = to require

knead = to work (dough) with hands

kneed = past tense of *knee*

net = open fabric; anything made from this fabric

nett or **net** = after deductions; final, ultimate

new = not old

knew = past tense of *know*

night = dark time of day

knight = armoured man on horseback

nit = small insect

knit = to weave wool into fabric with two needles

not (negative word)

knot = tied part of rope; nautical mile

none = not any

nun = female monk

nougat /'noogah/ or /'nugət/ = white sweet

nugget = solid lump; piece of information

nought = zero

naught = nothing at all; **come to naught, set at naught**

o = exclamation used in poetry

oh = usual exclamation of surprise, etc

oar = tool for rowing

ore = source of metal

of = belonging to

've = have: *I should've gone too*

pail = bucket

pale = of light colour; **beyond the pale**

pain = discomfort

pane = glass in window

pair = two   **pare** = to trim   **pear** = fruit

pal = friend

pall (*noun*) = covering: *a pall of smoke*; (*verb*) = to cease to be interesting

palate = roof of mouth

pallet = portable storage platform

palette = artist's board for paint

passed = past tense of *pass*

past (*noun*) = time before now; (*adjective*) = gone by; (*preposition*) = passing

pastel (*noun*) = chalk or crayon; (*adjective*) = pale

pastille = sweet

peace = absence of war

piece = bit, part

peak (*noun*) = top; front of cap; (*verb*) = to reach highest point

peek = look

peal = ringing of bells; sound of laughter

peel = fruit skin

pedal (on bike)

peddle = to sell; **pedlar**

peer (*noun*) = member of nobility; person of same age or status; (*verb*) = to look

pier = seaside structure

pendant = jewellery

pendent = hanging

personal = relating to a person

personnel = staff, employees

perspective = artistic representation

prospective = probable, expected

petrol = fuel

petrel = sea bird

pigeon = bird

pidgin = language

pistol = gun

pistil = part of flower

place = position

plaice = fish

plane (*noun*) = aircraft; tool for smoothing wood; flat surface; kind of tree; (*verb*) = to glide through the air or over water; (*adjective*) = flat, smooth

plain = undecorated; simple; pure or unmixed; straightforward; clear; obvious; **plain sailing**

plum = fruit

plumb (*adjective*) = vertical; (*adverb*) = exactly; **plumb line**

pole = rod

poll = votes cast, election; **poll tax**

pool = pond; supply

pull = to drag

pore (*noun*) = hole in skin; **pore over** = to read carefully

pour = to flow out, tip out

poor = not rich

portion = helping, share

potion = drink containing medicine, poison, or a magic substance

practice (*noun*)

practise (*verb*)

pray = to say a prayer

prey = animal or bird hunted for food

precede = to go before

proceed = to begin or continue activity

premier = prime minister

premiere = first performance of film, etc

premise or **premiss** = logical proposition

premises = building

prescribe = to recommend, command

proscribe = to prohibit

principal (*adjective*) = main, chief; (*noun*) = chief person

principle = general rule

prize (*noun*) = award; (*verb*) = to value highly

prise = to lever or force: *prise open a box*

programme (used in all senses except computing)

program (used in computing)

prophecy (*noun*)

prophesy (*verb*)

prophet = person who prophesies

profit = money gained

prostate = gland in the body

prostrate = lying face down

put = to place or position; **putting the shot; shot-put**

putt = to hit a ball in golf or putting

queue = line of people waiting

cue =prompt for actor, etc; stick for playing snooker

quiet (*adjective*) = peaceful; (*noun*) = calm

quite = completely, fairly

rain = water falling from sky

rein (*noun*) = part of horse's harness; (*verb*) = to restrain

reign = to rule as monarch

racket = noise; illegal enterprise

racket or **racquet** = bat for ball games

raise = to make higher or louder

raze = to destroy

rap = to hit

wrap = to enclose

rapt = wholly absorbed   **rapped** = past tense of *rap*   **wrapped** = past tense of *wrap*

rational = logical, sensible   **rationale** /rashə'nahl/ = reason

read = to look at book, etc   **reed** = grass-like plant

real = actual   **reel** (*noun*) = dance; thing for winding thread round; (*verb*) = to be dizzy

rest = relaxation; others   **wrest** = to take by force

retch = to be sick   **wretch** = bad or unfortunate person;   **wretched**

review = criticism of book, etc; ceremonial display of troops   **revue** = theatrical entertainment

rhyme = poem or verse   **rime** = frost

right (*adjective*) = correct; just; opposite of *left*; (*noun*) = entitlement   **rite** = ceremony   **write** = to make letters

ring (*noun*) = round object; phone call; (*verb*) = to form a ring; to call on phone   **wring** = to squeeze water out of;   **wring one's hands**

road = place for driving on   **rode** = past tense of *ride*   **rowed** = past tense of *row*

role or **rôle** = part in play, film or activity   **roll** (*verb*) = to move along by turning; (*noun*) = rolling movement; something wound round; long deep sound; piece of baked dough

rote (as in *learn by rote*)   **wrote** = past tense of *write*

root = origin; part of plant

route /root/ = way travelled

rout /rowt/ = overwhelming defeat

rough = not smooth; violent; approximate

ruff = collar; type of bird

row (*noun*) = line; (*verb*) = to use oars

roe = fish eggs; type of deer

rung (*verb*) = past participle of *ring*; (*noun*) = step of ladder

wrung = past participle of *wring*

rye = grain; whiskey

wry = ironically humorous

sale = selling

sail (*noun*) = part of boat; (*verb*) = to go by boat

sceptic /'skeptik/ = doubter

septic /'septik/ = infected

secret (*adjective*) = not told to others; (*noun*) = something not told

secrete /si'kreet/ = to hide; to produce and discharge

see = (*verb*) to have sight of; (*noun*) = district ruled by bishop

sea = ocean; large crowd

seed = what grows into a plant

cede = to yield, surrender

seem = to appear

seam = join in material

seen = past participle of *see*

scene = part of play; view

seer = person who predicts future

sear = to scorch

sew = to stitch

soh or **so** = musical note

sow = to plant seeds

shear = to clip (sheep)

sheer = complete; vertical; very thin

shoe = cover for foot

shoo = to chase away

sign (*noun*) = indication; indicator; (*verb*) = to write name

sine = ratio of side to hypotenuse

singing = present participle of *sing*

singeing = present participle of *singe*

slay = to kill

sleigh = sledge

slight (*adjective*) = little; (*noun*, *verb*) = insult

sleight (as in *sleight of hand*)

slow = not fast

sloe = berry

soar = to fly high

sore = painful

sole (*noun*) = fish; bottom of shoe; (*adjective*) = only

soul = spirit

some = a few

sum = adding; total

son = male child

sun = star

soot = black chimney dust

suit (*noun*) = clothes; set of cards; (*verb*) = to look right, be appropriate

suite /sweet/ = set of rooms; set of furniture; piece of music

staid = dull, unadventurous

stayed = past tense of *stay*

stair = steps up and down

stare = fixed look

stationary = not moving (★ *parked cars* are *stationary*)

stationery = paper, pens, etc (★ *stationery* includes *paper*)

staunch = strong, faithful

stanch = to stop flow of blood

steak = meat (★ *steak* is *meat*)

stake = pointed post; money gambled; share

steal = to take illegally (clue: *stealing* is *illegal*)

steel = metal

step = pace; part of stair

steppe = grassland

story = tale

storey = floor of building

straight = not curved; honest

strait = narrow channel; **dire straits; straitjacket; strait-laced; straitened circumstances**

sty = pigpen

stye or **sty** = swelling on eyelid

style = fashion, elegance; manner

stile = step over wall or fence

suite = set of rooms; set of furniture; piece of music

sweet = sugary; nice

summary = short version

summery = like summer

Sunday = day of week

sundae = ice cream

surplus = extra, remainder

surplice = gown

swat = to hit an insect

swot = to study hard

swinging = present participle of *swing*

swingeing = great, severe

symbol = sign

cymbal = musical instrument

tail = part of animal

tale = story

taught = past tense of *teach*

taut = tight

tea = drink; meal

tee (in golf)

team = players

teem = to exist in large amounts; to rain

tear /teer/ = drop of liquid from eye

tier = row

tear /tair/ = rip

tare = weight; plant

teeth = plural of *tooth*

teethe = to get teeth

tenor = male voice; character, trend

tenure = employment; conditions of occupation

their = of them   **there** = not here   **they're** = they are

threw = past tense of *throw*   **through** = from one side to the other

throws = present tense of *throw*   **throes** = difficult situation

tick = sound of clock; moment; mark of correctness; small insect   **tic** = muscle contraction

time = past, present and future   **thyme** = plant

toe = part of foot   **tow** (*verb*) = to pull; (*noun*) = fibre for spinning

> *They went and told the sexton, and*
> *The sexton toll'd the bell.*
> Thomas Hood, 'Faithless Sally Brown'

told = past tense of *tell*   **tolled** = rang bell

ton = 2240 pounds   **tonne** = 1000 kilograms   **tun** = barrel

too = also; excessively   **two** = pair, couple   **to** = in the direction of, etc

trail = path   **trial** = court case; difficult situation

troop (*noun*) = crowd; company; (*verb*) = to go in a crowd;
  troops = soldiers   **troupe** = group of entertainers

tray = flat board for carrying things   **trait** /tray/ or /trayt/ = characteristic

tyre (on wheel)   **tire** = to become tired

urban = of towns   **urbane** = cultivated, sophisticated

vain = proud; unsuccessful

vane = blade of propeller, etc

vein = blood tube; layer of ore; distinctive quality

veil = face covering

vale = valley

veracity = truthfulness

voracity = great appetite

waist = middle of body

waste (*noun*) = rubbish; desert; (*verb*) = to use carelessly

wait = stay

weight = heaviness

want = need, desire

wont /wohnt/ = habit

won't = will not

wave = movement of water; movement of hand

waive = to not insist on a claim or right

way = method; path;
  under way

weigh = to have weight; to find weight of;
  weigh anchor;
  (of ship) **under weigh**

weak = not strong

week = seven days

wear (*verb*) = to have on (as clothing); to damage by rubbing; (*noun*) = clothing: *underwear*; *nightwear*; damage;
  wear and tear

ware = goods; dishes: *earthenware*; *tableware*

weather = snow, rain, etc

wether = male sheep

whether = if

wet = damp

whet = to sharpen;
  whet someone's appetite

which (asking for information)

witch = female wizard

while = during   wile = trick

who's = who is: *Guess who's*   whose = of whom: *You're*
coming to the party!   *the one whose name is on the*
                                  letter.

wit = humour   whit = a little bit

wood = timber; trees   would (*verb*)

wreath (*noun*)   wreathe (*verb*)

yoke = collar for oxen, etc   yolk = yellow part of egg

you (person)   yew = tree   ewe = female
                                         sheep

your = of you   you're = you are   yore = long ago:
                                         days of yore

6

Spelling problems and spelling rules: vowels

The entries in this chapter are of two kinds:
1. Articles that draw attention to the difficult and un-predictable spellings of the various vowel sounds of English.
2. Articles that explain the main English spelling rules affecting vowels.

English vowels

English accents differ in the number of their vowel
sounds. For example, a standard southern British
accent has 20 vowels, but there are only 14 different
vowels in Scottish English.

For this reason, the vowel sounds will not be
considered individually but in groups of similar or
related sounds: the 'a' sounds /a/ and /ah/; the 'o'
sounds /o/, /oh/ and /aw/; and so on. In this way,
differences between accents that are irrelevant to
spelling can be ignored.

'a' sounds: /a/ and /ah/
Spellings to note are:

- *aunt*, *draught*, *laugh*; *heart*, *hearth*, *hearty*; and *clerk*,
  derby, *sergeant* (but with a short form *sarge*)
- words with a silent *l*: *almond*, *almoner*, *alms*, *balm*,
  balmy, *calm*, *napalm*, *palm*, *psalm*, *qualm*, *salmon*;
  behalf, *calf*, *half*, *calve*, *halve*
- words that end in *ah*: *hurrah*, *shah* (note also the
  spellings of *cheetah*, *hallelujah*, *hookah*, *loofah*,
  maharajah, *messiah*, *pariah*, *rajah*, *savannah*); also
  Fahrenheit
- words from French spelt *oi*: *boudoir*, *bourgeois* and
  bourgeoisie, *chamois*, *coiffeur* and *coiffure*, *memoir*,
  patois, *repertoire*, *reservoir*, *soiree*
- other unexpected spellings: *aardvark*, *bazaar*; *Gaelic*;
  diaphragm; *plaid*, *plait*; *impasse*, *lingerie*, *meringue*,
  timbre; and *reveille*

ae or *e*

In words that can be spelt both *ae* and *e*, British English generally retains the *ae* spelling, while in American English *e* is standard:

British English: *anaemia, anaesthetic, haemoglobin, haemorrhage, leukaemia, paediatrician*
American English: *anemia, anesthetic, hemoglobin, hemorrhage, leukemia, pediatrician*

However, *medieval* is now more common than *mediaeval* in British English, and *encyclopedia* is as common as *encyclopaedia*.

Aegis is the only correct spelling in both British and American English.

Aeon is commoner than *eon* in both British and American English, but both spellings are considered correct.

'ay' sounds: /ay/ and /air/

Spellings to note are:

- words spelt *ei*: *beige, feint, heinous, obeisance, rein, reindeer, surveillance, veil, vein*; and with a following *r*: *heir, heiress, their*
  A few words in this group also have silent letters: *deign, feign, reign; eight, freight, inveigh, neigh, neighbour, sleigh, weigh, weight*
- words spelt *ey*: *abeyance, convey, grey* (in British English; *gray* is the American spelling), *obey, prey* (= food), *purvey, survey, whey*
- *laid* and *paid*
- /air/ words with a final *e*: *billionaire, commissionaire,*

doctrinaire, millionaire, questionnaire (note also the double *n*), *solitaire*

- words that end in *ere*: *there, where; ampere, compere, premiere*
- words derived from Greek with an *aer-* spelling: *aerial, aerobics, aerodrome, aeronautics, aeroplane, aerosol*
- words taken from French, often spelt with accents (see page 283): *attaché, blasé, café, cliché, communiqué, consommé, fiancé, glacé, habitué, naïveté, protégé, résumé, risqué, sauté, soufflé; entree* (or *entrée*), *fricassee, matinee, melee* (sometimes *mêlée*), *negligee, puree* (or *purée*), *soiree* (or *soirée*), *toupee*; in two cases there is a difference in spelling to match a difference in gender: masculine *fiancé, protégé*, feminine *fiancée, protégée*

    Also: *cortege* (or *cortège*), *crepe* (or *crêpe*), *fete* (or *fête*), *suede* (very rarely *suède*)
- also from French, words with a silent *t, r* or *z*: *ballet, beret, bouquet, buffet, cabaret, chalet, crochet, croquet, duvet, gourmet, ricochet, sachet, tourniquet, valet; dossier, foyer; laissez-faire, pince-nez, rendezvous*
- other spellings: *Gaelic, maelstrom, sundae; champagne, campaign, straight; dahlia; halfpenny; gaol* and *gaoler; gauge*

/e/

Spellings to watch are:

- words spelt with *ea*: *bread, breadth, breakfast, breast, breath, deaf, death, head, health, heaven, heavy, instead, leather, pleasant, pleasure, ready, steady, sweat, treacherous, treasure; wealth, weapon, weather,* etc

★ word-families may act as reminders: *break, break-fast; breathe, breath; clean, cleanliness, cleanse; heal, health; heave, heavy; please, pleasant, pleasure; treason, treacherous; steal, stealthy*

★ verbs that are spelt *ea* in the present tense also have *ea* in the past tense: *dream, dreamt; leap, leapt; mean, meant* (whereas verbs spelt *ee* in the present tense have *e* in the past tense: *keep, kept; sleep, slept*)

- words derived from Greek: *aesthetic* (and also *anaesthetic*), *haemorrhage, haemorrhoids* – think of this *ae* spelling as the 'Greek /e/'
- other spellings: *said, again, against; debt* (★ related to *debit*); *phlegm* (★ related to *phlegmatic*); *heifer, leisure; jeopardy, leopard; friend; lieutenant; bury* and *burial*

e-dropping

e-dropping is the loss of a final *e* in words such as *brake, guide, ice,* etc when a word-ending beginning with a vowel (such as *-ing, -able* or *-ance*) is added:

brake > braking   *debate > debatable*
guide > guidance   *ice > icy*

The *e* is not usually dropped before a consonant:

manage + ment > management
white + ness > whiteness
extreme + ly > extremely

Another type of *e*-dropping is seen in some words that end in *er* when a suffix beginning with a vowel (such as *-ess* or *-ance*) is added:

tiger > *tigress*
hinder > *hindrance*
monster > *monstrous*

Final e followed by a vowel

When a word-ending that begins with a vowel is added to a word that ends in *e*, the *e* is generally dropped:

chase + ing > *chasing*   *change + ed* > *changed*
pursue + er > *pursuer*   *lie + ar* > *liar*
guide + ance > *guidance*   *interfere + ence* > *interference*
deplore + able > *deplorable*   *collapse + ible* > *collapsible*

and similarly:

haste, hasty   *rare, rarity*
erase, erasure   *legislate, legislation*
desire, desirous   *culture, cultural*
style, stylist   *purple, purplish*

Exceptions:

* The *e* is retained before a suffix beginning with *a* or *o* when it is needed to keep a preceding *c* or *g* 'soft' (that is, pronounced /s/ or /j/):

  change + able > *changeable*
  peace + able > *peaceable*
  courage + ous > *courageous*

* A final *e* is retained before *-ing* in order to distinguish between words that might otherwise be confused:

  sing, singing but *singe, singeing*

  Similarly:

  routeing, swingeing, tingeing, whingeing

Some people also keep the *e* in relatively uncommon words, e.g. *beigeish, mauveish*, but there is no need for this.

- Nouns and verbs ending in *ee*, *oe* or *ye* generally keep the final *e* before any letter except *e*:

agree + ing > agreeing   *agree + able > agreeable*
canoe + ing > canoeing   *canoe + ist > canoeist*
dye + ing > dyeing   *dye + able > dyeable*
absentee + ism >
 absenteeism

but:

agree + ed > agreed   *dye + er > dyer*

Oboist (= oboe-player) breaks this rule.
    Words ending in *ue* generally drop the *e* (*argue > arguing*, etc), but short words may optionally retain it:

cueing or *cuing*   *gluing* or *glueing*
queuing or *queueing*

- Verbs ending in *ie* change the *ie* to *y* before -*ing*:

die + ing > dying   *lie + ing > lying*
tie + ing > tying

- In a few words, a final *e* may be retained before *y*. Where there are two possible forms in the following list, the generally preferred form is given first:

cagey or *cagy*   *caky* or *cakey*
chocolaty or *chocolatey*   *cliquey* or *cliquy*
dicey   *dopey* or *dopy*

gluey	*holey*
horsy or *horsey*	*mangy* or *mangey*
matey or *maty*	*mousy* or *mousey*
nosy or *nosey*	*pacy* or *pacey*
pricey or *pricy*	*ropy* or *ropey*
samey	*smiley*
stagy or *stagey*	*winey* or *winy*

- Some one-syllable words may retain the *e* before the ending -*able*:

likeable/likable	*loveable/lovable*
sizeable/sizable	

There is a simple rule of thumb to apply:

If the vowel of the core word is a 'long vowel' (see page 308), then it is correct to keep the *e* (though forms without the *e* may also be correct):

blame, blameable or *blamable*	*like, likeable* or *likable*
move, movable or *moveable*	*name, nameable*
rate, rateable or *ratable*	*sale, saleable*
shake, unshakeable or *unshakable*	*size, sizeable* or *sizable*
tame, tameable or *tamable*	*tune, tuneable* or *tunable*

If the vowel is a 'short vowel', prefer the form without *e* (though forms with *e* are also correct):

give, givable or *giveable*	*live, livable* or *liveable*
love, lovable or *loveable*	

Note also *probable* (= 'likely') and *probeable* (= 'able to be probed').

- Some other words can be written with or without the *e*:

ageing or *aging*   *ageism* or *agism*
eyeing or *eying*   *knowledgeable* or
                                  knowledgable
mileage or *milage*

(In all these, the forms with the *e* are generally preferred.)
And *acreage* is always written with an *e*.

   Note also that this *e*-dropping rule does not apply to compound words, e.g. those formed from phrasal verbs:

giveaway, hideout, takeaway, takeoff, takeover, etc

Final e *followed by a consonant*
When a suffix beginning with a consonant is added to a word that ends in *e*, the *e* is usually not dropped:

move + ment > movement   *grace + ful > graceful*
polite + ness > politeness   *use + less > useless*
safe + ly > safely

and similarly:

tire, tiresome   *wave, wavelike*
false, falsehood   *lecture, lectureship*
bore, boredom

Exceptions:

- *judgement* or *judgment*   *acknowledgement* or
                                  acknowledgment
  (The forms with *e* are generally preferred.)

fledgling or *fledgeling*

(The form without *e* is generally preferred – but it would make sense to opt for the form with the *e*, and then you avoid an exception to the rule.)

Note also that many personal names and place-names break the general rule (*Bridgnorth, Bridgwater, Edgware, Hodgkin, Sedgwick, Wedgwood,* etc), though there are also names that retain the *e* (*Bridgewater, Bridgetown, Sedgemoor,* etc).

- *awe + ful > awful*   *argue + ment > argument*
  due + ly > duly   *true + ly > truly*
  eerie + ly > eerily   *whole + ly > wholly*
  nine + th > ninth   *while + st > whilst*
  wise + dom > wisdom

- When *-ly* is added to adjectives that end in *le* preceded by a consonant, simply replace the *e* with *y*:

  double + ly > doubly   *probable + ly > probably*

  And similarly:

  legibly, nobly, simply, possibly, predictably, subtly, visibly, etc

  (*Supplely* is preferred to *supply* because of possible confusion with the verb *to supply*.)

Final er *followed by a vowel*

A few words ending in *er* drop the *e*, and then only when certain word-endings (*-ance, -ess, -ous, -y*) are added:

encumber + ance > encumbrance   *enter + ance > entrance*
hinder + ance > hindrance   *remember + ance >*
                                      remembrance

hunter + ess > huntress　　　　*tempter + ess > temptress*
tiger + ess > tigress　　　　　*waiter + ess > waitress*
warder + ess > wardress

disaster + ous > disastrous　　*monster + ous > monstrous*

anger + y > angry　　　　　　*enter + y > entry*
hunger + y > hungry　　　　　*launder + y > laundry*
swelter + y > sweltry　　　　　*winter + y > wintry*
　　　　　　　　　　　　　　(but *wintery* is also correct)

Note that there are similar words that do *not* drop the *e*. For example:

suffer + ance > sufferance
cancer + ous > cancerous　　　*slander + ous > slanderous*
rubber + y > rubbery　　　　　*spider + y > spidery*

Perhaps the best way to deal with this problem is to spell the words as you say them. Say the words slowly to yourself, and *listen* to see if there is a missing *e*.

With other word-endings (such as *-ed* or *-ing*), the *e* is not dropped:

hinder + ed > hindered　　　　*remember + ing >*
　　　　　　　　　　　　　　　remembering

When *ess* replaces part of another word, the *e* is not dropped:

adulterer + ess > adulteress　　*murderer + ess > murderess*

'ee' sounds: /ee/ and /eer/

Spellings to watch are:

- words spelt *ei* or *ie* (see *ei* or *ie* on page 107)
- three words spelt with *ey*: *eyrie, geyser, key*
- *speak* and *speech*; *scream, screech* and *shriek*
- the large group of words (many of French origin) spelt with *i*: *chic; quiche; prestige; fatigue, intrigue, migraine; automobile, imbecile; regime; albino, ballerina, cuisine, guillotine, machine, magazine, margarine, marine, quarantine, ravine, routine, sardine, submarine, tambourine, tangerine; antique, boutique, clique, critique, mosquito, mystique, oblique, physique, pique, technique, unique; expertise; elite, graffiti, litre; kiwi,* etc
- scientific and medical words spelt *-ine* or *-ene*: *glycerine, morphine, nicotine, quinine, strychnine, vaccine; acetylene, benzene, ethylene, gangrene, kerosene, methylene, phosgene, polythene, terylene*
- plurals ending in *ae*: *antennae, formulae,* etc
- nouns ending in *eer* and *ier*: most end in *eer*, e.g. *auctioneer, charioteer, commandeer, mountaineer,* etc, but *bombardier, brigadier, cashier, cavalier, chandelier, frontier, fusilier, gondolier, grenadier, vizier*
- other spellings: *aegis, aeon* (often *eon*), *anaemia, archaeology, encyclopaedia* (or *encyclopedia*), *haemoglobin, mediaeval* (now usually *medieval*), *quay; amoeba, diarrhoea, foetus, oesophagus, people, phoenix* and *subpoena*

ei or *ie*

'I before E except after C' is a spelling rule that many of us learned at school. The rule is, however, not quite as simple as it is stated, and needs to be broken down into several separate rules.

Rule 1

The rule 'I before E except after C' strictly applies only to words that are pronounced /ee/.

After any consonant but *c*, the spelling is *ie*:

brief, chief, field, fiend, fierce, grief, hygiene, liege, niece, piece, pier, pierce, priest, reprieve, retrieve, shield, shriek, siege, thief, tier, wield, yield, etc

After the letter *c*, the spelling is *ei*:

ceiling, conceive, conceit, deceive, deceit, perceive, receive, receipt

Exceptions: *caffeine, codeine, protein, seize, weir* and *weird*. Note in particular *siege* and *seize*, which are often misspelt.

NAMES

Some personal names and place-names disobey the general rule:

Keith, Neil, Sheila, Reid
Madeira

Rule 2

After a *c* or a *t* pronounced /sh/, the spelling is *ie*:

ancient, conscience, efficient, patience, species, sufficient, etc

(★ *Conscience* is related to *conscientious* and *science*, in which the *ie* spelling is obvious. This is the key clue for the whole group.)

Rule 3

Before an *r*, the spelling for the sound /ie/ is *ie*:

fiery, hierarchy, hieroglyphics

(★ The vowels in *fiery* and *fire* are in the same order, *i* then *e*. This is the key to this group.)

Rule 4

In other cases where the sound of the vowel is not /ee/, the spelling is almost always *ei*:

beige, deign, eight, feign, foreign, forfeit, freight, heifer, height, leisure, neighbour, reign, rein, skein, vein, weigh, weight, etc

This applies also to words that have another pronunciation in addition to /ee/:

counterfeit, either, heinous, inveigle, neither, sheikh

Exceptions: *friend, mischief, sieve.*

GERMAN SPELLING
In words of German origin, the vowel sound /ee/ is always spelt *ie* and /ie/ is spelt *ei*:
Liebfraumilch, lieder
Fahrenheit, leitmotif, Weimaraner

/i/

The main spelling problems lie with the large group of words of Greek origin in which the sound /i/ is spelt *y* (the 'Greek /i/'): *abysmal, abyss, analysis, bicycle, crypt, crystal, cygnet, cylinder, cynic, dynasty, embryo, hymn, hypnotism, hypocrite, hysterical, larynx, misogyny, mystery, mythology, nymph, onyx, oxygen, paralysis, physical, physics, physiology, sycamore, syllable, symbol, system, tyranny* etc; also *tryst*.

There are certain spelling patterns worth noting:

- technical words that begin with /sil/, /sim/ or /sin/ are likely to be spelt with a *y*: *syllable, syllabus, symbol, symmetry, sympathy, symphony, symptom, synchronize, syndicate, syndrome, synonym*
- technical and scientific words that begin with /hip/ or /his/ are likely to be spelt with *y*: *hypnotism, hypocrite, hysteria, hysterical*
- scientific words beginning with /fiz/ are likely to be spelt *phys*: *physician, physics, physiology*
- the 'mysterious and mythical' group of words: *mysterious, mystery, mystic, mystical, mysticism, mystify, mystique, myth, mythology*; also *cryptic*

- grammatical terms that end in *nym*: *acronym, antonym, homonym, synonym,* etc
- *poly* meaning 'many': *polyester, polygamy, polyglot, polygon, polymer, Polynesian, polystyrene, polytechnic, polythene, polyunsaturated,* etc
  (★ Word-families sometimes help: *cycle, bicycle; analyse, analysis, analyst, analytic; tyrant, tyrannous, tyranny.*)

  Other /i/ spellings to note are:

- words ending in *ey*: *abbey, alley, chimney, donkey, hockey, honey, money, monkey, trolley, turkey, valley,* etc
- words ending in *ie*: *auntie, brownie, budgie, calorie, cookie, hankie, lingerie, menagerie, movie, nightie, pixie, prairie,* etc (see page 213)
- words (of foreign origin) ending in *i*: *bikini, broccoli, chilli, confetti, corgi, graffiti, Jacuzzi, khaki, macaroni, muesli, Nazi, safari, salami, scampi, spaghetti, taxi*
- words in which /i/ at the end of a word is spelt *e*: *acne, anemone, apostrophe, catastrophe, epitome, facsimile, finale, forte, furore, karate, machete, posse, recipe, simile, ukulele, vigilante*
- *college, privilege, sacrilege; knowledge*
- three words ending in *feit*: *counterfeit, forfeit, surfeit*
- other unexpected spellings: *breeches, busy* and *business, lettuce, minute* (= 60 seconds), *sieve*

ie changing to *y*
Verbs that end in *ie* change this *ie* to *y* when the suffix *-ing* is added:

belie + ing > belying   *die + ing > dying*
lie + ing > lying   *tie + ing > tying*
vie + ing > vying

Exception: the archaic verb *hie* is a partial exception to this rule as both *hying* and *hieing* are considered correct.

Die *and* dye

Distinguish carefully the correct spelling of the parts of the verbs *die* and *dye*:

die, dying, dies, died
dye, dyeing, dyes, dyed

'ie' sounds: /ie/ and /ire/

Spellings to note are:

- words with a silent *gh*: *high, nigh, sigh, thigh*; *alight, blight, bright, delight, fight, flight, fright, knight, light, might, night, plight, right, sight, slight, tight, wright*; *brighten, lighten,* etc
- words with a silent *g*: *paradigm*; *assign, design, resign, sign* (★ word-families provide some clues: *paradigm, paradigmatic*; *assign, assignation*; *design, designation*; *resign, resignation*; *sign, signature*)
- words spelt with final *i*: *alibi, alkali, hi-fi, pi, rabbi*; plurals such as *alumni, cacti, fungi, Gemini, gladioli, Magi,* etc
- words ending in *ai*: *assegai, bonsai, samurai, shanghai*
- words with a 'Greek *y*' (though not all of Greek origin): *asylum, cyanide, dynamic, hyacinth, hybrid,*

hyena, hygiene, hyphen, lychee, pylon, thyroid, tryst, typhoid, tyrant, etc

- words formed with *gyno-, gyro-, hydro-, hyper-, hypo- psycho-, xylo-, -lyse*
- words spelt *ye* or *y*—*e*: *dye, rye, stye* (in the eye); *byre, lyre, pyre, tyre; cycle, enzyme, rhyme, style, thyme, type,* etc (watch out for *die/dye, tire/tyre,* etc)
- words spelt *ei*: *eider, eiderdown, Fahrenheit, kaleidoscope, poltergeist, seismic; either, neither; height, sleight* (as in 'sleight of hand' in conjuring)
- other spellings: *aisle, isle* and *island; maestro*

'o' sounds: /o/, /oh/ and /aw/

Spellings to note are:

- words with *a* before *l*: *alter, bald, falcon, false, halt, salt,* etc
- words with *au* before *l*: *assault, cauldron, cauliflower, fault, somersault, vault*
- words with a silent *l*: *chalk, stalk, talk, walk*
- words with *a* after /w/: *qualify, quality, quarrel, quarter, squabble, squash; dwarf, swallow, swan, swat* (= 'hit'), etc; *walrus, walnut, waltz, war, warbler, warm, warn, wart, wharf,* etc
- words spelt *au*: *applause, assault, auburn, autumn, because, cauldron, cauliflower, cause, cautious, exhaust, fault, fauna, flaunt, flautist, fraud, gaunt, haunt, launch, laundry, nausea, pause, sauce, sauna, saunter, sausage, somersault, taut, vault,* etc; *centaur, dinosaur*

  Words with *au* plus a silent *gh*: *caught, daughter, distraught, fraught, haughty, naught, onslaught, slaughter, taught*

- words with *ou*: *boulder, mould, moult, poultice, poul-try, shoulder, soul*, etc; *course, court, mourn, pour, source*, etc

    Words with *ou* plus a silent *gh*: *bought, brought, fought, nought, ought, sought, thought, wrought; dough, though* (note also *cough* and *trough*)
- words with final *ow* or *o*: *arrow, barrow, blow, borrow, bungalow, crow, flow*, etc
    alto, avocado, banjo, bingo, buffalo, cargo, casino, cello, echo, embryo, halo, hero, judo, kilo, mango, motto, proviso, salvo, solo, studio, trio, veto, volcano, etc

    ★ Notice that *o* comes at the end of words relating to, for example, music (*alto, banjo, cello, solo, tango, tempo, trio*) and food (*avocado, potato, mango, tom-ato*), and in short forms (*photo, kilo*)
- words ending in 'French /oh/ spelt *eau*': *beau, bureau* (note also *bureaucrat* and *bureaucracy*), *chateau, gateau, plateau, portmanteau, tableau*
- words of French origin with final *ot*: *argot, depot, escargot, Huguenot, tarot*
- French words with *en* or *an*: *détente, encore, ensem-ble, entourage, entrepreneur, rendezvous; blancmange*
- other spellings: *knowledge* and *acknowledge* (★*know*); *sew* (with thread); *yeoman; ohm; folk* and *yolk; brooch, door* and *floor; chauffeur, gauche* and *mauve; wrath* (= anger) and *wroth* (= angry); *yacht; gone* and *shone*; and (for some people) *lingerie*

o-dropping

When the suffix *-ess* is added to a word ending in *-or*, the *o* is generally dropped:

actor + ess > actress   *ambassador + ess >*
                                   ambassadress

benefactor + ess > benefactress *editor + ess > editress*

instructor + ess > instructress *proprietor + ess > proprietress*

protector + ess > protectress   *sculptor + ess > sculptress*

Exceptions: *authoress, mayoress*. Note also *empress, sed-uctress*.

Note, however, that most of these *-ess* forms have now mostly dropped out of use:

> *I'm an actor. An actress is someone who wears boa feathers.*
>
> Sigourney Weaver

oe or *e*

There are only a few words in this category, fortunately, as current usage is a little confused.

The simple cases are *diarrhoea* and *oesophagus*:

British English *diarrhoea, oesophagus*
American English *diarrhea, esophagus*

Note the following:

- *Amoeba* is the form used in British English, and also in American English except in technical writing, where *ameba* is the preferred form.
- In both British and American English, the spelling *fetid* is preferred to *foetid*.
- Until recently, the standard British spelling was *foetus*, the American spelling *fetus*. But in British English *fetus* is now the preferred form in technical writing.

'oo' sounds: /oo/, /ooh/ and /oor/
Spellings to watch are:

- words spelt with *eu*: *adieu, deuce, feud, leukaemia, lieu, milieu, neuter, neutral, pneumatic, pseudo, neurology, rheumatism, sleuth, therapeutic,* etc; *eulogy, euphoria, euthanasia,* etc (words from Greek, with the underlying notion of something 'good': see page 220); *beauty* and *beautiful, manoeuvre, liqueur* (all from French)
- words spelt with *ou* (many of French origin): *boudoir, boulevard, bouquet, bourgeois, boutique, coupon, courier, denouement, goulash, group, gourd, gourmet, mousse, ragout, rendezvous, rouge, roulette, route, routine, silhouette, souvenir, troupe,* etc
- words spelt with *ou* plus a silent *l*: *could, should, would*; or a silent *gh*: *through*
- words spelt *ui*: *bruise, cruise, fruit, juice, nuisance, pursuit, recruit, sluice, suit*
- one word with a silent *g*: *impugn* (★ related to *repugnant*)
- other spellings: *canoe, shoe*

Be careful with the spelling of *prove* and *proof*, and of *lose* and *loose*. Take care also not to confuse homonyms such as *blue/blew, fool/full, pool/pull, to/too/two, troop/troupe,* etc.

'ow' sounds: /ow/ and /our/
Spellings to watch are:

- words with *ou* plus a silent *gh*: *bough, doughty, drought, plough*

- one word with *ou* plus a silent *b*: *doubt*
- one other spelling: *sauerkraut*

Take care with homophones such as *fowl* (= bird) and *foul* (= bad), and *flower* and *flour*, and with words that have similar sounds but different spellings, such as *blouse* and *browse*.

/oy/

The basic rule is that you write *oi* before a consonant (*boil*, *loin*, *noise*, *rejoice*, etc) and *oy* at the end of a word or before a vowel (*employ*, *joy*, *loyal*, *soya*, etc).

The basic *oy* spelling does not change when a word-ending is added: *employment*, *joyful*.

Exceptions to watch are:

- foreign words such as *borzoi* and *hoi polloi*
- *boycott*, *gargoyle*, *oyster*

/u/

Spellings to watch are:

- the large group of words in which /u/ is spelt with an *o*: *brother*, *mother*, *nothing*, *other*, *another*, *smother*; *accomplice*, *accomplish*, *among*, *colour*, *comfort*, *comfortable*, *company*, *compass*, *conjuror*, *constable*, *front*, *govern*, *Monday*, *money*, *mongrel*, *monk*, *monkey*, *month*, *onion*, *son*, *sponge*, *ton*, *tongue*, *won*, *wonder*, *wonderful*, *worry*; *become*, *come*, *covenant*, *cover*, *covet*, *covey*, *done*, *dove*, *dozen*, *glove*, *love*, *lovely*, *-monger* (*fishmonger*, *ironmonger*), *none*, *once*, *one*, *oven*, *plover*, *shove*, *shovel*, *slovenly*, *somersault*, etc; note also *does* (from *to do*)

- words spelt with *ou*: *country, couple, courage, cousin, double, enough, flourish, nourish, rough, southern, touch, tough, trouble, young,* etc; and with a silent *gh*: *borough, thorough*
- two words spelt *oo*: *blood, flood*

/ur/

For many people, words such as *berth* and *birth*, *fur* and *fir*, *earn* and *urn*, and *curb* and *kerb* have the same vowel sound, which in this book has the phonetic symbol /ur/. This causes many spelling problems.

Spellings to watch are:

- words spelt with *er*: *confer, defer, infer, prefer, refer, transfer; deter, inter; berth, concerto, disperse, fern, fertile, gherkin, herd, kerb, immerse, perfect, permanent, kernel, nerve, serge, serve, swerve, verse, verve;* and *err*
- words with *ear*: *dearth, earl, early, earn, earnest, earth, heard, hearse, learn, pearl, rehearse, search, yearn*
- words of French origin spelt with *eur*: *chauffeur, connoisseur, entrepreneur, masseur, raconteur, restaurateur* (not *✗restauranteur*); also unstressed in *grandeur*
- words with *ir*: *bird, birch, birth, chirp, circle, circus, dirge, first, girder, girl, irk, shirt, sir, skirmish, skirt, squirm, squirt, stir, third, thirteen, thirty, virtual, virtue, whirl;* words beginning with *circum-*; and with *rr*: *whirr*
- words spelt *or*: *attorney, word, world, worm, worse, worship, worst, worth, worthy*
- words spelt with *our*: *courteous, courtesy* (do not confuse *courtesy* and *curtsy*), *journey*

- words spelt with *yr* and *yrr*: *myrtle, myrrh*
- one odd spelling: *colonel* (formerly spelt *coronel*, which explains the pronunciation)

Take particular care with the spelling of the homonyms such as *kerb* and *curb*, *heard* and *herd*, etc.

★ One way to handle these /ur/ words is to learn them in groups: *nerve, serve, swerve, verve; earn, learn, yearn;* etc.

★ Word-families also help: for example, *heard* is the past tense of *hear*, *herd* is related to *shepherd*.

★ You can also make up memory aids with words that have the same spelling:

He furtively put the furs and the furniture in the furnace.
The herd preferred the gherkins and the kernels to the fertile ferns.
There were thirty birds in the birches and the firs.
Have you heard about the dearth of pearls?

y changing to *i*
y before a vowel
RULE 1

If a word ends in a consonant plus *y*, the *y* changes to *i* before a suffix beginning with *a, e* or *o* (for example *-able, -age, -al, -ed, -er, -est, -ous*):

carry, carriage, carried, carrier
cry, cried, crier
marry, marriage, married
rely, reliable, reliant, relied
try, trial, tried, trier
vary, variable, variant, variation, varied, various
frosty, frostier, frostiest

Exceptions:

Some short words (*dry*, *fly*, *fry*, *shy*, *sly*, *spry*, *wry*) break the general rule. Most allow inflections and derivatives with both *y* and *i* spellings, but the forms with *y* are generally preferred (and not all authorities accept all the *i* forms as correct):

dryer or *drier* (as a noun – the comparative adjective is always *drier*)
flyable, *flyer* or *flier*
fryer or *frier*
shyer or *shier*, *shyest* or *shiest*
slyer or *slier*, *slyest* or *sliest*
spryer, *spryest*
wryer or *wrier*, *wryest* or *wriest*

RULE 2
Before a suffix beginning with the letter *i*, *y* remains *y*:

carry, carrying	*vary, varying*
baby, babyish	*forty, fortyish*
copy, copyist	*lobby, lobbyist*
entry, entryism	*Tory, Toryism*

RULE 3
If the *y* is preceded by a vowel, it remains *y* before all vowels:

betray, betrayal, betrayed, betrayer, betraying
convey, conveyance, conveyed, conveying, conveyor
employ, employed, employee, employer, employing
play, playable, played, player, playing

Exceptions:

- *lay, laid; pay, paid; say, said*
- Adjectives ending in *ey* (such as *cagey, clayey, dicey, gooey, matey, pricey*) change the *ey* to *i* before *er* and *est*:

  cagey, cagier, cagiest   *gooey, gooier, gooiest*

- Both *moneyed* and *monied* are correct.

y *before a consonant*
RULE 1

A *y* following a consonant at the end of a word changes to *i* before the suffixes *-less, -ly, -ment, -ness* and *-some*:

mercy, merciless   *pity, pitiless*
penny, penniless

cosy, cosily   *easy, easily*
funny, funnily

merry, merriment

hairy, hairiness   *manly, manliness*
sleepy, sleepiness

weary, wearisome   *worry, worrisome*

Exceptions:

- *Busyness* is spelt with a *y* to distinguish it from the related word *business* /ˈbiznɪz/.
- With *-ly* and *-ness*, certain short words (*dry, shy, sly, spry* and *wry*) break the general rule. The following forms are generally considered correct (though not

by all authorities), with the preferred form given first:

drily or *dryly*; *dryness*
shyly or *shily*; *shyness*
slyly or *slily*; *slyness*
spryly; *spryness*
wryly; *wryness*

With *-ful*, the final *y* changes to *i* in an *adjective* but not in a *noun*:

beauty, beautiful   *duty, dutiful*
mercy, merciful   *plenty, plentiful*
belly, bellyful   *caddy, caddyful*

With *-hood*, the final *y* of an *adjective* changes to *i*, but not that of a *noun*:

hardy, hardihood   *likely, likelihood*
baby, babyhood   *puppy, puppyhood*

Note also the spelling of *livelihood*.
   With other endings, the *y* remains *y*:

twenty, twentyfold   *lady, ladyship*
baby, babykins

Note the spelling of *manifold*.

RULE 2
Before the ending *-s*, *y* becomes *ie*:

cry, cries   *lady, ladies*
spy, spies   *pony, ponies*
rely, relies   *soliloquy, soliloquies*

Exceptions:

- Proper names usually keep the *y* before -*s*:

  the two Germanys   the four Marys
  the Emmys (= 'the Emmy Awards')

but:

  the Kingdom of the Two Sicilies

- The plural of *poly* (= polytechnic) is *polys*.
- The final *y* in a compound noun does not change to *ie*:

  lay-bys   stand-bys
  Johnny-come-latelys

- When a word is being referred to in a sentence rather than being an integral part of the sentence, *y* does not change to *ie*, and the ending is often preceded by an apostrophe:

  There are too many possiblys (or possibly's) in his plan.

RULE 3
If the *y* is preceded by a vowel, it remains *y*:

boy, boyhood, boys   coy, coyly, coyness
play, playful, plays   valley, valleys

Exceptions:

- The plural of *money* may be *moneys* or *monies*.
- Adjectives ending in *ey* change the *ey* to *i* before -*ly*:

  cagey, cagily   matey, matily

- Authorities disagree over the correct spellings of nouns formed by adding *-ness* to adjectives ending in *ey*. A good rule is to keep the *ey* spelling when *ey* follows a vowel but change *ey* to *i* when it follows a consonant (including *y*):

  gluey, glueyness   gooey, gooeyness
  matey, matiness   nosey, nosiness
  clayey, clayiness

  However: *samey, sameyness*. No good authorities accept *✗saminess* as correct.
- Note *daily* and *gaily*.

7
Spelling problems and spelling rules: consonants

The main problems with consonants are:

- sounds that can be spelt in different ways (e.g. *back, bloc, trek, plaque*)
- the choice between single and double letters (e.g. *accommodation* and *accumulation, civility* and *tranquillity*)
- silent letters (as in *almond* and *phlegm*), which will be described more fully in Chapter 10.

/b/
Spellings to watch are:

- the double *b* of *abbreviate* and *abbreviation* (see ***Single and double letters in words of Latin and Greek origin***, page 157)

- the double *b* in inflections and derivatives such as *grabbed* and *grabbing*, *ribbed* and *ribbing*, *robbed*, *robber* and *robbing* (see *Single and double consonants in inflections and derivatives*, page 147)
- the single *b* in words such as *cabin* and *robin* as opposed to the double *b* in words such as *cabbage*, *ribbon* and *rubbish* (see also *-ic, -id, -ish, -it*, page 134); also *treble* and *trouble*, etc but *pebble* and *bubble*, etc (see *Single and double consonants: the 1–2/2–1 rule*, page 164)
- the silent *u* in *build*, *buoy* and *buy*
- the silent *b* in *comb*, *crumb*, *debt*, *doubt*, *subtle*, etc (see page 229)

ce or *se* at the end of a word
Words with a final /s/ sound may be spelt with either a *c* or an *s*:

fence, pence but *sense, tense*
commerce but *endorse*
peace but *lease*

Most of the spellings cannot be predicted, but rules of thumb cover some cases.

Rule 1
When /s/ follows /ie/ or /oy/, it will be spelt with a *c*:

advice, device, lice, mice, slice, vice, etc
choice, invoice, rejoice, voice, etc

If /s/ follows /ow/, it will be spelt with an *s*:

grouse, house, louse, mouse, etc

Rule 2

Nouns related to adjectives ending in *-ant* and *-ent* are always spelt with a *c*:

dominant, dominance	*ignorant, ignorance*
evident, evidence	*violent, violence*

Similarly with other words derived from verbs:

guidance, interference, reference, etc

The same holds true for words ending in *y*:

accountant, accountancy	*decent, decency*
urgent, urgency	

Rule 3

Licence and *practice* are nouns, *license* and *practise* are verbs. (The same distinction holds for the noun *prophecy* and the verb *prophesy*.)

   Defence, offence and *pretence* are spelt with a *c*. The corresponding adjectives are spelt with an *s*:

defensive, offensive

(American spellings are slightly different: see Chapter 18.)

Rule 4

Adjectives are generally spelt with an *s*:

coarse, hoarse; close; loose; dense, immense, intense, tense; diverse, terse; worse; obtuse, profuse

But note *fierce, nice* and *scarce*.

Rule 5

There are several verbs that end in *-duce*:

deduce, induce, introduce, produce, reduce, seduce, etc

★ These words are all derived from Latin. Thanks to Latin grammar, the word-family gives a clue to the *c* spelling:

deduce, deduction   *introduce, introduction*
produce, production

No rule

For the rest of the words ending in /s/, there is no discernible rule.

Among the words spelt with *c* are:

advance, commence, commerce, dance, fence, finance, fleece, force, hence, juice, justice, malice, office, palace, pence, piece, pierce, place, police, pronounce, romance, sauce, since, truce

Among the words spelt with *s* are:

abuse, base, case, cease, course, crease, chase, geese, goose, grease, horse, lapse, lease, moose, noose, purpose, refuse, release, response, sense

Note also the spelling of *controversy*.

/ch/
ch *or* tch?

Some words are spelt *ch*: *approach, bench, brooch, church, much, teach, which,* etc. Other words are spelt *tch*: *blotch, butcher, catch, ditch, fetch, kitchen, match, notch, satchel, scotch, watch,* etc. The rules are fairly straightforward, though there are a few exceptions.

RULE 1
If the /ch/ sound is preceded by a consonant sound, it will be spelt *ch*:

belch, bench, branch, crunch, filch, finch, ranch, squelch, zilch, etc

RULE 2
If what precedes the /ch/ is a vowel sound spelt with two or more letters, /ch/ will be written *ch*:

beach, brooch, coach, couch, debauch, leech, smooch, screech, teach, touch, etc

Rules 1 and 2 apply whether or not you pronounce *r*'s in this position:

arch, church, march, lurch, perch, search, torch, etc

Exception: *aitch.*

RULE 3
If /ch/ is preceded by a vowel sound written with a single letter, it will be spelt *tch*:

butcher, catch, dispatch, fetch, hitch, hutch, kitchen, latch, satchel, watch, witch, wretch, etc

Exceptions:

attach, bachelor, detach, macho (and *machismo*), *spinach*
lecher, lecherous, etc
enrich, ostrich, rich, sandwich, which (and in some people's
 pronunciation *lichen*)
duchess, duchy, much, such
lychee or *lichee, lychgate* or *lichgate*

> **NAMES**
> Some names are exceptions to Rule 3:
>
> *Richard*
> *Bromwich, Greenwich, Harwich, Lichfield, Norwich,*
> *Richmond, Sandbach, Sandwich, Tichborne, Wisbech,*
> *Woolwich,* etc

Other spellings

Other spellings of /ch/ to watch are:

- words of Italian origin: *cello, concerto, vermicelli*
- words from Chinese: *ch'i* or *qi, ch'i kung* or *qi gong, t'ai chi ch'uan* or *tai ji quan* (other spellings are frequently seen, especially *chi, chi kung* and *tai chi chuan,* but, although in common use, they are not strictly speaking correct)

/d/

Spellings to watch are:

- the double *d* of words of Latin and French origin such as *addict* and *address* (see *Single and double letters in words of Latin and Greek origin,* page 157)
- the double *d* in inflections and derivatives such as *bidding, gladden, muddy, sadder* (see *Single and double consonants in inflections and derivatives,* page 147)
- the double *d* in *muddle, paddle, sudden* and single *d* in *beadle, treadle, wheedle,* etc (see *Single and double consonants: the 1–2/2–1 rule,* page 164; see also *-ic, -id, -ish, -it,* page 134)

- the silent *d* in *grandma, handkerchief, handsome* and *sandwich,* and (for many people) *landscape*
- the single *d* of *grandad* (*granddad* is also correct)
- the silent *h* of *dhow,* and of *Buddha* and *Gandhi* (frequently misspelt)

Double consonants in words with prefixes or suffixes

A **prefix** is a word-forming element that is added to the beginning of a word to make a new word:

possible > impossible	*sane > insane*
behave > misbehave	*understand > misunderstand*
paid > prepaid	*recorded > prerecorded*
able > unable	*known > unknown*

A **suffix** is a word-forming element that is added to the end of a word either to form a new word or to add grammatical information to a word (present tense, past tense, plural, etc):

quick > quickly	*slow > slowly*
harm > harmless	*home > homeless*
hope > hopeful	*pity > pitiful*
sing > sings	*write > writes*
clap > clapped	*talk > talked*
cat > cats	*house > houses*

When a prefix or suffix is added to a word, it may sometimes happen that two identical letters are juxtaposed:

dis + satisfied = dissatisfied	*dis + similar = dissimilar*
il + legal = illegal	*il + legitimate = illegitimate*

im + material = immaterial	*ir + regular = irregular*
mis + spell = misspell	*mis + spent = misspent*
un + necessary = unnecessary	*un + natural = unnatural*
actual + ly = actually	*real + ly = really*
lean + ness = leanness	*sudden + ness = suddenness*

This should pose no spelling problems, but misspellings such as ✗*disimilar*, ✗*ilegal*, ✗*unecessary*, ✗*actualy*, ✗*realy* and ✗*drunkeness* are very common. To avoid such spelling mistakes, simply think about the meaning and structure of the words, when the need for the double letters will be quite clear.

Note, however, that English spelling does not permit *three* identical consonants together, and to avoid this one consonant is dropped:

dull + ly > dully	*full + ly > fully*
shrill + ly > shrilly	

See also **Single and double consonants in inflections and derivatives** on page 147.

If a prefix such as *dis-* or *mis-* is added to a word beginning with a vowel, there is, of course, no need for a double letter: you simply tack on the prefix to the beginning of the word:

dis + appear = disappear	*dis + appoint = disappoint*
in + edible = inedible	*in + elegant = inelegant*
mis + interpret = misinterpret	*mis + understand = misunderstand*

/f/

Spellings to watch are:

- the double *f* in words such as *affair, affect, affirm, different, difficult, effect, efficient, offend, offer, official, sufficient,* etc (see *Single and double letters in words of Latin and Greek origin,* page 157)
- the double *f* in words such as *baffle, daffodil, giraffe, graffiti, paraffin, raffle, scaffold, traffic; bailiff, plaintiff, sheriff, sniffle, tariff; coffee, coffin, toffee, waffle; buffalo, buffoon, dandruff, ruffian, snuffle,* etc (see *Single and double consonants: the 1–2/2–1 rule,* page 164)
- the single *f* in words ending in *ific* and *ify: horrific, prolific, scientific, specific, terrific,* etc; *horrify, specify, terrify,* etc (see also *-ic, -id, -ish, -it,* page 134)
- words with *gh: cough, draught, enough, laugh, rough, tough, trough*
- words of Greek origin with *ph: cenotaph, diaphragm, dolphin, epitaph, euphoric, metaphor, paraphernalia, paraphrase, phenomenon, phrase, prophet, sophisticated*; words formed with *-graph, photo-, philo-, phono-, phys-*; also *sapphire*
- *lieutenant*

/g/

Spellings to watch are:

- the double *g* in words of Latin origin: *aggravate, aggressive, aggrieved,* etc (see *Single and double letters in words of Latin and Greek origin,* page 157)
- the double *g* in many words in inflections and derivatives: *bigger, foggy, logging, sagged,* etc (see

Single and double consonants in inflections and derivatives, page 147)

- the double *g* in *giggle, haggle, smuggle, wiggle, wriggle, juggernaut, skulduggery*, etc (see **Single and double consonants: the 1–2/2–1 rule**, page 164)
- words spelt g*h*: *ghastly, gherkin, ghetto, ghost, ghoul, aghast, dinghy, spaghetti, yoghurt* (*yogurt* is also correct)
- words beginning *gu*: *guarantee, guard, guardian, guerrilla, guess, guest, guide, guild, guile, guillemot, guillotine, guilt, guinea, guise, guitar, guy*
- words ending in *gue*: *colleague, fatigue, intrigue, league, morgue, plague, rogue, vague, vogue; catalogue, demagogue, dialogue, monologue, synagogue* (*catalog, dialog*, etc are correct only in American English)
- words in which *x* = /gz/: *auxiliary, exaggerate, exam, example, exasperated, exhaust, exist*, etc

/h/

The sound /h/ causes few problems. Silent *h* is more of a problem. Spellings to watch are:

- words with initial *wh*: *who, whom, whose, whole, whoop* (for some speakers), *whooping cough* (for most speakers), *whore*
- words with a silent *h*: *heir, heiress, honest, honour, hour; dahlia, jodhpurs, myrrh, silhouette, vehement; exhibit* and *exhibition, exhilarate, forehead* (for many speakers), *philharmonic, shepherd, vehicle* (★ for this last group, word-families provide clues from words in which the *h* is pronounced: compare *inhibit, hilarity, head, harmony, herd, vehicular*); *catarrh, diarrhoea,*

haemorrhage (these all have the *rrh* word element (see page 226)
- *cheetah, mynah, rajah,* etc (see page 96)
- *ohm*

-ic, -id, -ish, -it

A useful rule of thumb for dealing with some of the problems of single and double letters is the following: the word-endings -*ic* (also -*ical* and -*ics*), -*id*, -*ish* and -*it* are generally preceded by a single consonant:

academic, acrobatic, alcoholic, angelic, athletic, atomic, botanical, chronic, comic, dramatic, economic, epic, epidemic, ironic, manic, mechanic, organic, physical, physics, static, telescopic, tonic, topical, tropical, etc

acid, avid, florid, insipid, intrepid, invalid, rabid, rapid, rigid, solid, timid, valid, vivid, etc

abolish, astonish, banish, blemish, cherish, demolish, diminish, famish, finish, parish, polish, punish, radish, vanish, etc

credit, debit, deficit, habit, illicit, limit, merit, prohibit, solicit, spirit, vomit, etc

Exceptions:

- *attic, classic, metallic, traffic, tyrannical*
  horrid, pallid
  embellish, rubbish
  rabbit, summit
- words formed with the -*ish* that means 'sort of': *biggish, clannish, reddish, snobbish,* etc (see page 149)

/j/

Spellings to watch are:

- words of Latin origin with a double *g*: *exaggerate*, *suggest*; and words with *dj*: *adjacent*, *adjective*, *adjourn*, *adjudicate*, *adjunct*, *adjust*, *adjutant*, etc (see **Single and double letters in words of Latin and Greek origin**, page 157)
- words with initial *g*: *gel*, *gelatine*, *gem*, *gender*, *gene*, *general*, *generate*, *generous*, *genius*, *gentle*, *germ*, *giant*, *gill* (= quarter pint), *gin*, *ginger*, *giro*, *gist*, *gym*, *gypsy*; words beginning with *geo-* and *gyro-*
- words with *g* in the middle: *agile*, *digit*, *fragile*, *imagine*, *largesse*, *logic*, *magic*, *pageant*, *pigeon*, *refrigerator* (but short form *fridge*), *rigid*, *tragic*, *turgid*, *vegetable*, *vigil*, *vigilance*, *vigilante*; words ending in *-logy*, *-logical*, *-logist*
- words ending in *ge*: *allege*, *carriage*, *college*, *coverage*, *heritage*, *leverage*, *marriage*, *message*, *passage*, *privilege*, *sacrilege*, *verbiage*, etc
- words spelt with *dg*: *badge*, *badger*, *cadge*, *gadget*, *dredge*, *edge*, *fledge*, *hedge*, *knowledge*, *ledger*, *pledge*, *bridge*, *fidget*, *fridge*, *midget*, *dodge*, *lodge*, *stodgy*, *budge*, *budgerigar* (and *budgie*), *budget*, *cudgel*, *grudge*, *judge*, *nudge*, *trudge*, etc (see page 160 for more about *g* and *dg*, and page 103 for the lack of *e* in *fledgling*, *judgment*, etc)
- *margarine*

/k/

In common words, *k* often comes before an *e* or an *i*: *keep, key, kill, kind, king*, etc. *C* comes before *a, o* and *u*: *can, carry, come, cool, cub, cuddle. K* most often comes before *a, o* or *u* in words of foreign origin: *kamikaze, karate, koala, kowtow, kung fu*.

Spellings to watch are:

- words of Latin origin spelt with *cc*: *acclaim, accommodation* (often misspelt), *accompany, accomplish, account, accumulate* (often misspelt), *accurate, accuse, occult, occur*, etc; also *accent, accept, accident, eccentric, succeed, vaccine, vaccinate*, etc (see **Single and double letters in words of Latin and Greek origin**, page 157)

- other words with *cc*: *broccoli, buccaneer, desiccate, moccasin, peccadillo, piccolo, saccharine, soccer, staccato, tobacco, yucca, zucchini*, etc, but note *macaroni*

- final *ck* versus *k* after a vowel: *brick, crack, stock*, etc but *break, croak, shriek*, etc (see **Single and double consonants: the 1–2/2–1 rule**, page 164); some words, especially words of foreign origin, do not obey the general rule: *amok, kayak, kapok, trek, wok, yak; bloc, chic, frolic, maniac, picnic, sac, tic, traffic* and short forms such as *choc* and *doc*

- words ending in *c* which add a *k* before a suffix: *picnic, picnicking, traffic, trafficker*, etc (see **Single and double consonants in inflections and derivatives**, page 147)

- words spelt with initial *sc* or *sk*: *scald, scale, scan, scar, sceptic* (American spelling *skeptic*), *scone, scoop, score, scrap, scrape, screech, screw, script, scuffle, sculptor*, etc, but *skate, sketch, ski, sky, skull*, etc

- words (mostly of Greek origin) with *ch* for /k/: *archaic, archangel, architect, anchor, chameleon, chaos, character, charisma, chasm, chemist, chiropodist, chlorine, cholera, cholesterol, chorus, Christian, chromium, echo, epoch, eunuch, machismo, masochist, monarch, ochre, orchestra, sepulchre, stomach,* etc; *schedule* (for some speakers; originally an American pronunciation), *scheme, schism* (for some speakers), *schizophrenia, school, scholar, scholastic*; words with the word-elements *archae-, bronch-, chron-, psych-, tech-; ache* and *gnocchi*

- words with *c* and *ck* before *le*: *article, bicycle, chronicle, circle, cubicle, cycle, icicle, miracle, obstacle, oracle, particle, tentacle, testicle, treacle, uncle, vehicle,* etc, but *buckle, cackle, chuckle, cockle, crackle, fickle, freckle, knuckle, pickle, tackle, tickle, trickle,* etc

- words with /k/ followed by /w/: *adequate, banquet, conquest, eloquent, frequent, inquest, inquiry, marquis, qualm, quarantine, quarter, quick, quiet, quit, quite, quiz, quote, tranquil, turquoise,* etc, but *choir, coiffure* and *cuisine*; for the spelling of *acquaint, acquire, acquit,* see **Single and double letters in words of Latin and Greek origin**, page 157)

- words (mostly from French) with *qu* for /k/: *bouquet, communiqué, conquer, croquet, etiquette, liqueur, liquor, marquee, mosquito, tourniquet,* etc; *brusque, cheque, clique, opaque, pique, plaque, quay, quiche, quoit,* etc; also words with the endings *-esque* and *-ique: burlesque, grotesque, picturesque,* etc; *antique, boutique, critique, mystique, oblique, physique, technique, unique,* etc; note also *lacquer*

- words with *xc* for /ks/ in: *exceed, excel, excellent,*

except, excerpt, excess, excise, excite; but note *ecstasy, eczema*

- words with a silent *h*: *gymkhana, khaki, saccharine, zucchini*
- *evoke, invoke, provoke, revoke* but *evocation, invocation, provocation, revocation*; *kleptomania*; *biscuit* and *circuit*; *recce* (from *reconnoitre*)

/l/
Final /l/
In a one-syllable word ending in /l/ in which the vowel sound is spelt with a single letter, /l/ will almost always be spelt with a double *l*:

ball, bell, call, doll, pull, roll, small, troll, etc

Exceptions: *gal, gel, nil, pal*.
    Other words ending in /l/ will have a single *l*:

ale, male, mile, mole, pale, pile, pole, tale, tile, etc
ail, boil, bowl, coal, feel, foul, jail, meal, pail, pool, real, soil, soul, etc
appal, appeal, distil, equal, final, initial, instil, retail, scandal, symbol, etc

Derivatives and compounds generally preserve the spelling of their base words:

call, recall	*fill, refill*
fall, pitfall	*mill, sawmill*

Exceptions:

null, annul	*roll, enrol*
stall, install or *instal*	*thrall, enthral*
till, until	

- Final *ll* loses one *l* when followed by any suffix begin-ning with a consonant, except *-ness*:

  dull + ly > dully   *full + ly > fully*
  skill +ful > skilful   *will + ful > wilful*
  install + ment > instalment
  smell/spell/spill + t > smelt/spelt/spilt
  full + some > fulsome
  thrall + dom > thraldom

  but:

  dull + ness > dullness   *ill + ness > illness*
  full + ness > fullness (fulness is an out-of-date spelling)

  Both *l*'s are retained before a suffix beginning with a vowel: *skilled, willing, smelled, spelling, duller, full-est,* etc

- *almighty, almost, already, altogether* (also *alright* – see page 52), *belfry, chilblain, fulfil, welfare*

For the doubling of *l* in derivatives (e.g. *council, coun-cillor; travel, travelling*), see page 152.

Other spellings
Other spellings to watch are:

- the double *l* in words of Latin origin: *allegation, alleviate, allocate, allusion, collect, colleague, collide, illuminate, illustrate, intelligent,* etc (see **Single and double letters in words of Latin and Greek origin**, page 157)
- single and double *l* in inflections and derivatives:

appalling, appealing, etc (see *Single and double consonants in inflections and derivatives*, page 147)

- the double *l* in words with the prefix *il*: *illegal, illegible*, etc (see *Double consonants in words with prefixes or suffixes*, page 130)
- words with single and double *l*: *balance, battalion, chalet, cholera, column, develop, lily, malice, palace, palate, palatial, pavilion, salad, salon, scholar, solemn, talent*, etc, but *alligator, allow, ballet, balloon, brilliant, bulletin, gallery, lollipop, million, parallel*, etc
- words that end in *le* or *al*: *apple, article, battle, bottle, candle, castle, circle, dazzle, feeble, fondle, gobble, middle, noble, paddle, single, sprinkle, subtle, table*, etc; and words ending in *-able* and *-ible*: *capable, eligible, formidable, intelligible*, etc

  (★ Words ending in *al* are often derived from other words: *appraisal, arousal, dispersal, disposal, proposal, recital, refusal, removal, reversal* from *appraise, arouse, disperse, dispose*, etc; *bridal, brutal, causal, central, digital, fatal, formal, historical, oriental, partial, principal, radical, spatial, spinal, substantial, thermal, tidal, universal* from *bride, brute, centre, digit, fate, form, history, part*, etc.

  Other common adjectives ending in *al*: *dental, dismal, final, initial, legal, lethal, marital, mental, vital*; other common nouns ending in *al* are *cymbal, festival, interval, mammal, marshal, medal, pedal, sandal, scandal, signal*.)

- nouns ending in *el*: *angel, brothel, camel, caramel, channel, chapel, colonel, counsel, flannel, funnel, enamel, kennel, marvel, morsel, panel, satchel, scoundrel, shovel*, etc

- nouns ending in *il*: *basil, council, pencil, stencil*
- nouns ending in *ol*: *gambol, idol, petrol, symbol* (★ *idolatry, petroleum, symbolic*)
- *principal* (= main) and *principle* (= rule); *counsel* (= advice) and *council* (= committee)
- words with a silent *l*: *could, should, would; calm, half*, etc; *talk, walk,* etc (see page 233)

/m/

Spellings to watch are:

- words of Latin origin with a double *m*: *accommodate, command, commence, comment, commerce, communicate, inflammable,* etc (see **Single and double letters in words of Latin and Greek origin**, page 157)
- words beginning with *im* (= 'not' or 'in'): *immanent, immaterial, immature, immeasurable, immediate, immigrant, imminent, immoral, immortal,* etc (see **Double consonants in words with prefixes or suffixes**, page 130)
- inflections and derivatives with a double *m*: *swimming, jammed, dimmer,* etc (see **Single and double consonants in inflections and derivatives**, page 147)
- words with silent letters: *bomb, climb, comb, almond, balm, salmon, diaphragm, paradigm, phlegm, autumn, column, damn,* etc (see page 228; ★ *paradigmatic, phlegmatic, autumnal, columnist, damnation,* etc)

/n/

Spellings to watch are:

- words of Latin origin with a double *n*: *annihilate, announce, annoy, annual, annuity, annul, connect, conniving, connotation, innocent, innate, innuendo, innocuous, innovation, perennial,* etc (see *Single and double letters in words of Latin and Greek origin,* page 157); note that *inebriated, iniquity, inoculate, inept, inexorable* and *inundate* only have one *n*

- derivatives with a double *n*: *winning, sinner,* etc (see *Single and double consonants in inflections and derivatives,* page 147)

- *banner, cannibal, cannon, cinnamon, spanner, tyranny,* etc with double *n*, but *canister, canon, cynical, sinister,* etc

- words with a silent *g*: *gnarled, gnash, gnat, gnaw, gnome, gnostic* (★ think of *agnostic*), *gnu; assign, benign, design,* etc (★ think of *assignation, benignant,* etc – see page 231); *align, campaign, champagne, cologne, ensign, foreign, physiognomy, reign, sovereign*

- words with a silent *k*: *knack, knapsack, knave, knead, knee,* etc (see page 232)

- other words with silent letters: *mnemonic, pneumatic, pneumonia*

- for many people, *government* with a silent *n* (★ think of *govern*)

- words of French and Italian origin in which /ny/ is spelt *gn*: *cognac, gnocchi, poignant, vignette*

/ng/

Spellings to watch are:

- words that end with *ngue*: *harangue*, *meringue*, *tongue*
- *handkerchief*, with a silent *d*

/p/

Spellings to watch are:

- words with a double *p*: *apparent*, *appeal*, *appear*, *apply*, *approach*, *appropriate*, *approve*, *oppose*, *oppress*, *suppose*, *supply*, *support*, etc (see **Single and double letters in words of Latin and Greek origin**, page 157); but single *p* in *apartment*, *apathy*
- words of Greek origin beginning with *apo-*: *apocalypse*, *apocryphal*, *apology*, *apoplexy*, *apostle*, *apostrophe*, *apothecary*
- double *p* in derivatives: *chopping*, *shopper*, *snapped*, etc (see **Single and double consonants in inflections and derivatives**, page 147)
- words with double and single *p*: *apple*, *copper*, *hippo*, *pepper*, *supper*, *supple*, etc, but *apart*, *chapel*, *proper*, *triple*
- words with a silent *p*: *cupboard*, *pneumonia*, *psychology*, *pterodactyl*, *raspberry*
- words in which (for some speakers) /p/ is spelt *ph*: *diphtheria*, *diphthong*, *naphtha*
- *hiccough* as a possible spelling of *hiccup*

/r/

Spellings to watch are:

- words of Latin origin with a double *r*: *arrange, arrest, arrogant, correct, correspond, corrupt, interrogate, surreal, surrogate,* etc (see **Single and double letters in words of Latin and Greek origin**, page 157)
- words beginning with *ir-* meaning 'not' or 'in': *irrational, irregular, irrelevant, irradiate, irrupt,* etc (see **Double consonants in words with prefixes and suffixes**, page 130)
- single or double *r* in inflections and derivatives: *offered, referred, furry,* etc (see **Single and double consonants in inflections and derivatives**, page 147)
- words with a single or double *r*: *apparel, baron, bury, carol, cherub, claret, coral, florist, foreign, forest, garage, herald, heron, mirage, moral, orange, peril, sheriff, tariff,* etc, but *barricade, barrister, corridor, garrison, horrify, narrative, terrapin, terrier, terrify, territory,* etc
- words with an initial silent *w*: *wren, wrestle, wrinkle, wrist, wrong,* etc (see page 235)
- words with initial *rh*: *rhapsody, rheumatism, rhino, rhubarb, rhyme,* etc (see page 232)
- words with the *rrh* word-element: *catarrh, diarrhoea, haemorrhage,* etc (see page 226); also *myrrh*
- words with the *-er, -or* and *-ar* endings: *leader, collector, liar,* etc (see page 191)
- words that end in *re* as opposed to *er*: *cadre, calibre, centre, fibre, litre, macabre, massacre, meagre, mediocre, mitre, ochre, ogre, sabre, sceptre, sepulchre, sombre, spectre* (most of these words are spelt *er*

in American English – see page 298); but note *meter* (= 'measuring instrument') and *metre* (= 'length')

- *colonel*

/s/

Spellings to watch are:

- words of Latin and French origin with an *ss*: *assault, assemble, assent, assert, asset, assimilate, assist, associate, assume, assure, dissipate, dissolute*, etc (see **Single and double letters in words of Latin and Greek origin**, page 157); also words in which *cc* is pronounced /ks/: *accelerate, accent, accept, access, accident, occident, success*, etc

- other words beginning with *dis-*, and with *mis-*: *dissimilar, misspell*, etc (see **Double consonants in words with prefixes and suffixes**, page 130)

- other words with double or single *s*: *ambassador, assassin, bassoon, brassiere, casserole, cassette, classic, classify, connoisseur, embassy, essential, gossip, massacre, mousse, potassium, reconnaissance, renaissance*, etc, but *aerosol, dinosaur, moccasin, unison*, etc

- words in which /s/ is spelt *sc*: *abscess, ascetic, ascertain, adolescent, ascent, crescent, descent, discern, disciple, discipline, fascinate, miscellaneous, obscene, omniscient, oscillate, rescind, resuscitate, scenario, scene, scenery, scent, sceptre, science, scimitar, scissors, susceptible, scythe*, etc

- words in which /s/ is spelt with a *c*: *bicycle, celebrate, celestial, celibate, cellular, cemetery, centre, cereal, ceremony, certificate, circular, cycle, cygnet, cylinder, cynical, hyacinth,* etc; and words beginning with *circum* and *cyber*

- words in which /ts/ is spelt *tz, z, or zz*: *blitz, chintz, ersatz, glitz, hertz, kibbutz, quartz, schmaltz, schnitzel, waltz*; *Nazi, scherzo, schizophrenia*; *intermezzo, mezzo-soprano, pizza*

- words ending in *ce* and *se*: *fence, tense,* etc (see page 125); words ending in *cy* and *sy*: *democracy, hypocrisy,* etc (see page 180); words ending in *city* and *sity*: *atrocity, capacity, curiosity, generosity,* etc (see page 201)

- words spelt with a silent *t*: *apostle, boatswain, bristle, castle, fasten, listen, moisten, waistcoat,* etc (see page 234); *muscle* with a silent c (★ *muscular*); *answer* and *sword* with a silent *w*; *asthma* and *isthmus* with silent *th*; *psalm* and *psalter* with silent *p*

- French words spelt with a 'cedilla' under the *c*: *aperçu, façade*

- *tsar/tzar/czar* (all correct); *schism* (for some speakers)

/sh/
Spellings to watch are:

- *ch* in words of French origin: *avalanche, brochure, cache, chagrin, chalet, champagne, chandelier, chaperon, charade, charlatan, chassis, chef, chemise, cheroot, chevron, chic, chiffon, chivalry, chute, cliché, cloche, crochet, crèche, douche, echelon, gauche, machine, marchioness, moustache, niche, nonchalant, panache, parachute, quiche, ricochet, sachet*

- words in which /sh/ is spelt *sc*: *conscience, conscientious, conscious, crescendo, fascist*

- words in which /sh/ is spelt *sch*: *Schadenfreude, schedule, schist, schmaltz, schnapps, schnitzel, schnozzle, schottische*
- the word endings *-sion* and *-tion*: *suspension, tension,* etc, but *discretion, erection, function, intention, section,* etc (see page 209); also *impression, passion, possession, recession, session,* etc (★ many of these are derived from verbs that end in *ss*: *impress, possess,* etc); note also *magician, technician,* etc (★ *magic, technical,* etc)
- *censure, commensurate,* etc (★ *sure*)
- words in which /sh/ is spelt *ci* or *ti*: *appreciate, officiate, official, racial,* etc, but *negotiate, palatial, spatial,* etc
- *fuchsia*

Single and double consonants in inflections and derivatives

Inflections and derivatives are formed by adding a suffix (such as *-al, -ed, -er, -est, -ing, -ly, -ness, -or* or *-s*) to a word in order to make a new word or a different form of the word:

quicken, quicker, quickest, quickish, quickly, quickness from *quick*
walked, walker, walking, walks from *walk*

Sometimes words change their spelling slightly when suffixes are added. For example, when a suffix beginning with a vowel is added to a word that ends in a single consonant, the consonant is sometimes doubled:

slip, slipped, slipping *stop, stopped, stopping*
fat, fatten *hot, hotter, hottest*
sad, sadden *red, redder, reddest*

In other cases, the final consonant is not doubled:

clean, cleaned, cleaning   *stoop, stooped, stooping*
dead, deaden   *tight, tighten*
green, greener, greenest

This causes many spelling problems, but the rules are fairly straightforward, though there are exceptions.

Rule 1
If the suffix begins with a consonant, the preceding letter is never doubled:

red, redness   *sad, sadly, sadness*
cup, cupful   *sin, sinful*
spot, spotless   *top, topless*
commit, commitment   *defer, deferment*

The following rules therefore apply only to suffixes beginning with *vowels* (e.g. *-able*, *-age*, *-al*, *-ance*, *-ed*, *-ence*, *-er*, *-ess*, *-ible*, *-ing*, *-ism*, *-or*, or *-y*).

Rule 2
If a suffix beginning with a vowel is added to a word in which the final consonant is preceded by two vowel sounds or a vowel sound spelt with two or more letters, the consonant is not doubled:

lion, lioness   *ruin, ruination, ruined, ruining*
triad, triadism
avoid, avoidance, avoided,   *moan, moaned, moaner,*
  avoiding   *moaning*
cheap, cheapen, cheaper,   *dream, dreamer, dreaming,*
  cheapest   *dreamy*

suit, suitable, suited, suiting *sweat, sweated, sweater,*
  sweating, sweaty

green, greener, greenest *leak, leakage, leaked, leaking*

fight, fighter, fighting *brown, browner, brownest*

Rule 3

If a suffix beginning with a vowel is added to a one-syllable word in which the final consonant is preceded by a vowel sound spelt with a *single* letter, the consonant is doubled:

bag, baggage, bagged, bagging, *sit, sitter, sitting*
  baggy

fat, fatten, fatter, fattest, fatty *hop, hopped, hopping*

grit, gritted, gritter, gritting, *god, goddess*
  gritty

sun, sunned, sunning, sunny

A *u* following a *q* counts as a consonant, /w/:

quit, quitter, quitting *squat, squatted, squatter,*
  squatting

The letter *x* is pronounced /ks/ and counts as two letters. It is therefore not doubled:

box, boxed, boxer, boxes, boxing

sex, sexed, sexes, sexing, sexy

Rule 4

This rule comes in two parts. The spelling of the derivative depends on which syllable of the base word is stressed; that is, which is the strongest or loudest syllable (compare, for example, *visit* and *offer* with stress

on the first syllable and *forget* and *occur* with stress on
the second syllable).

4a

In a word of more than one syllable, a final consonant
is doubled if the final syllable of the word is stressed
and the final consonant is preceded by a single vowel:

be'gin, beginner, beginning	*co'mmit, committed,*
	committee, committing
for'get, forgettable, forgetting	*o'ccur, occurred, occurrence,*
	occurring

4b

If the final syllable is not stressed, the final consonant
is not doubled:

'ballot, balloted, balloting	*'offer, offered, offering*
'open, opened, opener, opening	*'visit, visited, visiting, visitor*

---

consonant-doubling and e-dropping

Do not confuse the spellings of words in which there is
consonant-doubling and words in which there is
e-dropping (see page 99):

bar, barred, barring	*bare, bared, baring*
hop, hopped, hopping	*hope, hoped, hoping*
pin, pinned, pinning	*pine, pined, pining*
tap, tapped, tapping	*tape, taped, taping*

Refinements and exceptions

c

To preserve the /k/ sound of a final *c* before a suffix beginning with *e, i* or *y*, a *k* is added:

bivouac, bivouacked, bivouacking
colic, colicky
frolic, frolicked, frolicker, frolicking
garlic, garlicky
mimic, mimicked, mimicker, mimicking
panic, panicked, panicker, panicking, panicky
picnic, picnicked, picnicker, picnicking
tarmac, tarmacked
traffic, trafficked, trafficker, trafficking

Exceptions:

- *Talc* and *zinc* may add a *k*, but spellings without *k* are preferred:

  talced or **talcked, talcing** or *talcking, talcy* or *talcky*
  zinced/zincked/zinked, zincing/zincking/zinking, zincy/zincky/ zinky

- *Arc, chic* and *sync* (= *synchronize*) do not add a *k*:

  arc, arced, arcing
  chic, chicer, chicest
  sync, synced, syncing

- You do not, of course, add a *k* if the /k/ sound becomes /s/ or /sh/:

  critic, criticism, criticize   *electric, electrician, electricity*
  lyric, lyricist

- Nor is a *k* needed when the suffix begins with *a*, *o* or *u*:

  critic, critical   *electric, electrical*
  lyric, lyrical

fer

With words that end in *fer*, the final consonant is not doubled if the stress on the final syllable of the base word moves away from that syllable in the derivative:

con'fer, con'ferred, con'ferring but *'conference*
pre'fer, pre'ferred, pre'ferring but *'preferable, 'preference*
re'fer, re'ferral, re'ferred, re'ferring but *'reference, refe'ree*

but note the exceptions:

in'fer, in'ferable or *in'ferrable*
trans'fer, trans'ferable or *'transferable*

gram

Words ending in *gram* double the final *m* regardless of their stress pattern:

diagram, diagrammatic
program, programmable, programmed, programmer, programming

l

Words that end in *l* neither obey the basic rules consistently nor consistently break them. (American English spelling is slightly better than British English in this respect – see page 296.)

- If a final *l* is preceded by a single vowel sound written with two letters, the *l* is not doubled when a suffix is added:

appeal, appealed, appealing   fool, fooled, fooling, foolish
sail, sailed, sailing, sailor

Exceptions: *woollen, woolly.*

- When a final *l* is preceded by a single-letter vowel sound, it is doubled before most common suffixes (*-ance/-ence*, *-ation*, *-ed*, *-er/-or*, *-ery*, *-ing*, *-ion*, *-ious/-ous* and *-y*) *regardless* of the stress pattern of the base word:

a'ppal, appalled, appalling
re'bel, rebelled, rebelling, rebellion, rebellious
'cancel, cancellation, cancelled, cancelling
'council, councillor
'counsel, counselled, counselling, counsellor
'equal, equalled, equalling
'fuel, fuelled, fuelling
'gravel, gravelly
'jewel, jewelled, jeweller, jewellery
'libel, libelled, libelling, libellous
'marvel, marvelled, marvelling, marvellous
'signal, signalled, signaller, signalling

Exceptions:

- Before the suffixes *-ism, -ist, -ity* and *-ize/-ise*, the final *l* is usually not doubled:

civil, civility, civilize
equal, equality, equalize
final, finalist, finality, finalize
special, specialist, speciality, specialize

but:

crystal, crystalline, crystallize
panel, panellist
tranquil, tranquillity, tranquillize

Note also *tonsil, tonsillectomy, tonsillitis*.
- Two adjectives that end in *-ous* have only one *l*:

perilous, scandalous

One *l* is also the rule for adjectives that are not formed
by the direct addition of *-ous* to a word ending in *l*:

*anomalous, bilious, credulous, fabulous, garrulous, meticulous,
miraculous, nebulous, populous, querulous, ridiculous, scrupulous, scurrilous, supercilious*

- *parallel, paralleled, paralleling, parallelogram*

p

In British English, three words ending in a single *p*
double the *p* before a suffix contrary to Rule 4b:

handicap, handicapped, handicapping
kidnap, kidnapped, kidnapper, kidnapping
worship, worshipped, worshipper, worshipping

s

There are some words ending in *s* which allow both
single and double *s* in derivatives. In some, the doubling or non-doubling depends on whether the word is
being used as a noun or a verb:

bias   noun plural *biases*
          verb *biased* or *biassed, biasing* or *biassing*

bus   noun plural *buses* (also *busses* in American English)
         verb *bused* or *bussed*, *buses* or *busses*, *busing* or
         bussing

focus noun plural *focuses*
         verb *focused* or *focussed*, *focuses* or *focusses*, *focusing* or
         focussing

gas   noun plural *gases*
         verb *gassed*, *gasses*, *gassing*

plus   noun plural *pluses* or *plusses*
         (but for the verb *nonplus*: *nonplussed*, *nonplusses*,
         nonplussing)

yes   noun plural *yeses* or *yesses*

(If that seems too difficult to cope with, notice that a single *s* is always correct for the plural nouns, and a double *s* is always correct for the verb parts, even if not the preferred spelling: ★ single *s* in the noun, double *s* in the verb.)

t

There are a few words ending in *t* in which the *t* is, or may be, doubled in derivatives even when the preceding syllable is not stressed (contrary to Rule 4b). The following examples show the *-ed* and *-ing* derivatives, but the rule applies to other derivatives also:

benefit, benefited or *benefitted, benefiting* or *benefitting*
format, formatted, formatting
leaflet, leafleted or *leafletted, leafleting* or *leafletting*
photostat, photostatted, photostatting
ricochet, ricocheted /-'shayd/ or *ricochetted* /-'shetid/, *ricocheting*
  or *ricochetting*

Other words obey the general rule:

budgeted, budgeting; riveted, riveting; targeted, targeting; visited, visiting; etc

Silent letters
A final *h*, *w* or *y* that is part of a vowel is not doubled:

hurrah, hurrahed, hurrahing
allow, allowance, allowed, allowing
enjoy, enjoyable, enjoyed, enjoying

Other silent consonants (e.g. in words borrowed from French) are not doubled in derivatives:

pince-nez, pince-nezed /-nayd/
rendezvous, rendezvoused /-voohd/, *rendezvousing*

When a consonant is preceded or followed by a silent letter (as in *calm, talk* or *condemn*), there are two *written* consonants (although only one consonant is pronounced) and so the rule for doubling single consonants does not apply:

calm, calmed, calmer, calmest, calming
talk, talkative, talked, talker, talking
condemn, condemned, condemning

Compounds
Compounds keep the spelling of their final part regardless of the stress pattern of the compound:

step, stepped, stepping so *quickstep, quickstepped, quickstepping*
tan, tanned, tanning, so *suntan, suntanned, suntanning*
trot, trotted, trotting so *foxtrot, foxtrotted, foxtrotting*

whip, whipped, whipping so *horsewhip, horsewhipped, horsewhipping*

The same applies to a few words of a similar structure:

hobnob, hobnobbed, hobnobbing
humbug, humbugged, humbugging
leapfrog, leapfrogged, leapfrogging
zigzag, zigzagged, zigzagging

Note that there is no doubling of final letters *within* compounds:

get, getting but *getaway*
stop, stopped, stopping but *stopover*

Single and double letters in words of Latin and Greek origin

> *... but apart from the sanitation, the medicine, education, wine, public order, irrigation, roads, a fresh water system and public health, what have the Romans ever done for us?*
>
> *Monty Python's Life of Brian*

One other thing the Romans did is give English-speakers quite a lot of vocabulary. Unfortunately they also gave us a few spelling headaches. One of the worst of these is the problem of single and double letters in words like *accommodate* and *accumulate*, *immigrant* and *emigrant*, *offend* and *omit*.

il-, im-, ir-, dis-, syl-, *etc*

Some of the problems have been dealt with in *Double consonants in words with prefixes and suffixes* (see page 130). In words such as *illegible* and *dissimilar*, the double letters can be predicted from the structure and meaning of the words themselves:

dissimilar = *dis* + *similar* ('not similar')
dissymmetry = *dis* + *symmetry* ('lack of symmetry')
illegal = *il* + *legal* ('not legal')
illegible = *il* + *legible* ('not legible')
illicit = *il* + *licit* ('not licit, not allowed by law')
immature = *im* + *mature* ('not mature')
immigrant = *im* + *migrant* (an 'in-migrant')
immobile = *im* + *mobile* ('not mobile')
innumerable = *in* + *numerable* ('not numerable')
irregular = *ir* + *regular* ('not regular')

A NOTE ON ASSIMILATION

Assimilation is the name for the process by which a sound changes to become the same as, or in some way similar to, an adjacent sound. For example, in Latin and words derived from Latin, the prefix *in-* (= 'not') becomes *il-* before a following *l* (as in *illegal* and *illiterate*), *im-* before an *m* (as in *immature*) and *ir-* before an *r* (as in *irregular*). Similarly the prefix *in-* (= 'into') becomes *im-* before an *m* in *immigrant* (= an 'in-migrant').

There are, however, words in English whose structure and meaning are less obvious, because the main part of the word is not itself an English word: for example *immense, immaculate, immune, innocent, innocuous.* The need for the double *m* or *n* is therefore less evident.

To deal with the words in this category, you need to consider their meanings and structure, but for this you will have to consult your dictionary. For example, once you know that the *mense* part of *immense* comes from a Latin word meaning 'to measure', you can see that *immense* means almost the same as *immeasurable* (something that is *immense* is so big that you can hardly measure it), and you are well on the way to never forgetting how to spell it. Look up *immaculate, immune, innocent* and *innocuous* in your dictionary to see how the same principle applies.

Similarly, there are a number of words in English formed with *in-* = 'into' or 'onto': *illuminate* (= 'to shine light into or onto something'), *illusion, illustrate, illustrious, immerse, imminent, innovate* (= 'to bring in something new'), *innuendo, irrigate, irritate* and *irrupt.* In many cases the notion of 'into' or 'onto' is lost in modern English but a dictionary will again help you to understand the underlying meanings of the words and therefore the need for a double letter.

A dictionary will also explain why some words do *not* have a double letter. For example, *inoculate* and *inoculation* have this same *in-* = 'into' element, but there is only one *n* in these words because the Latin word underlying these words begins with *o*, not *n*: *inoculate* = *in-* + *oculate* (from Latin *oculus* 'bud'). Similarly, *inundate* is from Latin *unda* 'a wave' (a Latin word also seen in *undulating*).

Latin will also help you not to confuse *immigrant* and *emigrant*. In Latin, *e* means 'out of, away from'. So just as an *immigrant* is an *in-migrant*, an *emigrant* is an *e-migrant*, someone who migrates 'out of' a country. That is why there are two *m*'s in *immigrant* but only one *m* in *emigrant*. The same applies to *erupt* and *irrupt*, and to *eminent* and *imminent* (look up your dictionary to see why).

The same principle applies to words beginning with *dis-* = 'not', 'lacking' or 'the opposite of', or in some words = 'completely, widely', in which once again the need for a double *s* may not be obvious at first sight. Look up *dissect, dissemble, disseminate, dissent, dissertation, dissident, dissimulate, dissipated, dissolve* and *dissonant* in your dictionary and see how the meanings of the Latin roots of these words explain their meanings and point clearly to the need for the double *s*'s.

In two words, the *dis-* replaces another element: *dissociate* (compare *associate*) and *dissuade* (compare *persuade*).

Words of Greek origin, such as *syllable, syllabus, syllogism* and *symmetry*, are examples of the same phenomenon. The underlying element is Greek *syn-*, meaning 'with', which is found in *syndrome* and *synthetic* and (with assimilation of *n* to *m* before *b* and *p*) in *symbol, symphony, symptom*. The problem words are *syllable, syllabus, syllogism* and *symmetry*, where *syn-* has become *syl-* or *sym-* before a following *l* or *m* (for example, *symmetry* comes from *syn + metron*, the Greek word that gives us English *metre*). Again, your dictionary will help you to sort this out and remember it.

accommodation, aggression, *etc*

A large group of Latin-derived words give – at first sight – no clue whatsoever to the need for double letters: *abbreviate, accumulate, affiliate,* etc. For the most part, the English meanings of the words are of no help at all. What is necessary for successful spelling of the words in this group is, firstly, to know that the words *are* derived from Latin, and then secondly to recognize the Latin elements they are composed of.

The first thing, then, is to know that if a word ends in *-acy, -ate, -ation, -ence, -ent, -esce, -ible, -ion, -ition* or *-ity*, it almost certainly comes from Latin. Remember these endings – they are key spelling clues.

Secondly, you have to recognize common Latin word-forming elements, such as *ad-, com-, e-, in-, ob-* and *sub-,* and be aware that in Latin these word-forming elements undergo assimilation to a following letter (see the box on page 158).

Take, for example, the word-forming element *ad-* (meaning 'to') which we see in Latin-based words like *adhere* (= 'to stick to') and *adjoin* (= 'to be next to'). In Latin words, and in English words derived from Latin, *ad-* becomes *ab-* before a following *b, ac-* before a following *c, af-* before a following *f,* and so on. Thus we have *abbreviate* from *ad - breviate, accumulate* from *ad - cumulate, affiliate* from *ad - filiate,* and similarly *ag - gravate, ag - gression, al - locate, ap - preciate, ap - proximate, as - sociate, at - tention, at - traction,* all with an assimilated *ad- (as - similate* itself is an example of assimilation).

Any word, therefore, that is derived from Latin (which you recognize because it ends in *-ate, -ation,*

-*ion*, etc) and that begins with the sounds /ab/, /ak/, /af/ etc, will almost certainly have a double letter after the initial *a*.

But not always! This is not an absolutely foolproof rule, only a rule of thumb to help you find your way through one of the great difficulties of English spelling. There was also a Latin word-forming element *ab-*, and if *ab-* was followed by a vowel in Latin, you do not get a double consonant in English: *aberration, abolition, abomination, abortion*. You'll need your dictionary to check, but in fact there are few words in this group, so the general rule mostly applies.

Note also that before a /w/ sound you don't have a double *c* but *cq*, as in *acquisition*.

The same rule of thumb can be applied to words beginning with *col-, com-, con-* and *cor-*: *collaborate, collection, collision, collusion, commemorate, commiserate, connection, connotation, correction, correlation, correspondence, corrosion* and *corruption*. In some of these words we still see the original Latin word-forming element *com-* (meaning 'with'), and in others we see forms assimilated to a following consonant. But here again, when you recognize the Latin endings of these words, you can be pretty sure that you will need a double letter after the initial *co*.

Accommodation has both *ad-* and *com-* in it: *ac - com - modation*, hence the double *c* and the double *m*.
Accumulation has the underlying *ad-*, but what follows is *cumul* not *com*, so there is no double *m*.

Unfortunately, many English words do not have the key endings that are clues to their Latin origins (sometimes because they have come to us via French, sometimes for other reasons): *accord, account, appeal, appear, approach, assist, collect, collide, connect, correct, correspond, corrode, corrupt, acquaint, acquire, acquit,* etc. But word-families can help us: because we know that *acquisition, apparition, collection, collision, connection, correction, correlation, correspondence, corrosion, corruption* are Latin words and will therefore have double letters (or the *cq* spelling), we can be sure that there will be the same spellings in *acquire, appear, collect, collide, connect, correct, correspond, corrupt,* etc.

Two more Latin word-forming elements are *ob-* and *sub-*, again often found with assimilation, as in *occasion, occupy, occupation, occur, occurrence, offence, offend, offer, opponent, opportunity, oppose, opposite, opposition, oppress, oppression, succeed* (you can hear the double *c* here, as also in *success*), *suffer, sufficient, suffocate, suggest, suggestible, suggestion, supplement, supply, support, suppose, supposition, suppress, suppression.*

You should also note the double *f* in *differ, different, diffident* and *difficult,* which shows assimilation of *dis-* to a following *f.* And another double *f* is found in words in which Latin *ex-* (= 'out of') has also undergone assimilation to a following *f: effect, effeminate, effervesce, efficacy, efficacious, efficient, effluent, effort* and *effusive.*

Exceptions:

- Before an *m*, Latin had *e-* and *o-* instead of *ex-* and *ob-*. Hence we have *emigrant, eminent, emit* and *omit* with only one *m*. The same *e-* is found in words like *edition, eloquent, elude, emerge* and *emergency*.

- Some Latin word-forming elements ended in a vowel (e.g. *de-, pre-, pro-* and *re-*). They did not give rise to double consonants:

  deference, preference, reference, etc
  require, etc
  deposition, proposition, etc

Single and double consonants: the 1–2/2–1 rule

Look at the following pairs of words:

rubble, trouble	*supple, couple*
battle, beetle	
fiddle, poodle	*giggle, eagle*
worry, weary	*sorry, bleary*

Can you see the pattern? When the vowel sound is written with *one* letter, the following consonant sound is written with *two* letters (1–2), but when the vowel sound is written with *two* letters, the following consonant sound is written with only *one* letter (2–1). This is the '1–2/2–1 rule'.

Exceptions: *treble* and *triple*.

1–2/2–1 does not apply when there is more than one consonant sound after the vowel:

apple, ample	*cattle, candle*
rubble, rumble	

Nor does it apply when a vowel follows the consonant:

meddle but *medal, mettle* but *metal, peddle* but *pedal*

1–2/2–1 is a very important rule of English. Not only does it explain the spelling of words like the ones above, it also underlies the spelling patterns of inflections and derivations (see page 147):

sleep, sleeping	*slip, slipping*
green, greener	*red, redder*
stoop, stooped	*stop, stopped*
green, greenery	*pot, pottery*
dead, deaden	*sad, sadden*

The rule also applies to many short words:

sell, sail	*pull, pool*
fill, feel	
ruff, reef	*puff, beef*
black, bleak	*sick, seek*
screech, stretch	*peach, patch*
siege, sedge	

S and *z* are also double after a single-letter vowel:

less, mass, mess, miss, moss, pass, buzz, fizz, fuzz, jazz, etc (but *quiz* and *fez*)

Exceptions: *gal, gel, nil, pal.*

Other consonants do not follow the doubling rule:

club, knob, bed, rid, bag, clog, slim, pin, pit, clip, sip, box, fox, etc

But note *mat* and *matt*, *net* and *nett*, *pal* and *pall*, *put* and *putt* (see Chapter 5).

There are also words borrowed from other languages that do not obey this rule:

bloc, chef, clef, flak, trek, sac, tic, yak, etc

Note:

- *k* does not actually double but becomes *ck* after a single-letter vowel:

  black, brick, clock, rock, wreck, etc

- The letters *ch* represent a single consonant sound /ch/, and count as a single letter for the purposes of this rule. The 'doubling' of *ch* after a single-letter vowel is done by writing it as *tch*:

  blotch, catch, pitch, wretch, etc

  But note:

  much, rich, such, which, etc (see page 128)

- The 'doubling' of *ge* (= /j/) is done by writing *dge*:

  badge, edge, ridge, splodge, etc

Single and double consonants: the short and long vowel rule

It is not hard to find exceptions to the 1–2/2–1 rule:

griddle, bridle	*ruffle, rifle*
boggle, bugle	*apple, staple*
block, bloke	*wedge, wage*
comma, coma	

In each of these pairs of words, there is a single vowel letter, but whereas in some of the words the single vowel is followed by a double consonant (as the 1–2/2–1 rule would predict), in the other words the single vowel is followed by a *single* consonant, contrary to the rule. Are these words simply further exceptions to the rule?

Fortunately not. Rather than being exceptions to the 1–2/2–1 rule, they are examples of the **short and long vowel rule** (or **SLV rule**).

To understand the rule, you have first to understand the difference between what are traditionally called the 'short vowels' and the 'long vowels' of English (here, 'vowel' means 'vowel sound'). Quite simply, /a/, /e/, /i/, /o/, /oo/, /u/ and /ə/ are short vowels; all the others are long vowels.

Recognizing the difference between short vowel sounds and long vowel sounds allows us to explain the spellings of the words listed above. Short vowel sounds are followed by a double consonant:

griddle, ruffle, apple, boggle, comma, block, wedge

Long vowel sounds are followed by a single consonant:

bridle, rifle, staple, bugle, coma, bloke, wage

(Notice that a final *e* is often used in English to show that a preceding vowel is long: compare *sit* and *site*, *cap* and *cape*, *ton* and *tone*, etc.)

As a general rule, long vowels are not followed by double consonants; only short vowels are. There are many further examples of words in which there is a double consonant after a short vowel:

stubborn (compare the long vowel sound and single *b* in *tuba*)
copper, happen, pepper (compare *cupid, paper, stupid*)
barrel, barrow, borrow, ferry, sorrow (compare *fury, hero*)
kitten, mitten, latter, letter, matter (compare *later*)
dollar, follow, hallo, sullen, yellow (compare *halo, tulip*)
hammer, stammer (compare *tamer*)

dinner, manner, centennial (compare *centenary, tiny, tuna*)
bitten, litter, written (compare *writer*)
rudder (compare *ruder*)

There are, as you might expect, exceptions. For example, *driver* follows the rule, but *drivel* and *driven* do not. Nor does *shadow*. Compare also *manner* and *manor*, *batten* and *baton*, etc.

Single and double consonants: the three-syllables-from-the-end rule

The three-syllables-from-the-end rule explains the spelling of words such as *memory, regular, general, elephant, tolerate*, etc.

Syllables are the parts that words can be split up into in speech:

yellow has two syllables: *ye-llow*
elegant has three syllables: *e-le-gant*
centenary has four syllables: *cen-ten-a-ry*

In any word of two or more syllables, one syllable is always *stressed*, that is, spoken with more force than the others: '*ye-llow*, '*e-le-gant*, *cen-'ten-a-ry*.

According to the 'three-syllables-from-the-end rule', if the stressed syllable in a word is third from the end, and the vowel in the stressed syllable is a short vowel (see page 167), then the vowel is likely to be followed by a single letter:

cabinet, deliberate, elaborate, liberty, probable
chicory, faculty
academy, adamant, moderate
definite

bigamy
elegant, elephant, policy, tolerate
chemical, demonstrate, homicide, primitive, similar
economy, energy, generate, vinegar
citizen, strategy
lavender, privilege

This rule can, of course, also help with the spelling of related words in the word-families, even when the stress is not on the third syllable from the end:

liber'tarian, mode'ration, simi'larity, eco'nomic, ener'getic,
stra'tegic

Exceptions:

- Words formed from shorter words by the addition of a suffix:

  rob, robbery,   *rubber, rubbery*
  shrub, shrubbery

- Words that are covered by the rule explained in *Single and double letters in words of Latin and Greek origin* (see page 157):

  accommodate, arrogant, communist, difficult, innocent, etc

- Some other words, for example:

  broccoli, cannabis, hickory, moccasin, piccolo, possible

(These and others you come across should be noted in your spelling file as exceptions to the general rule.)

/t/

Spellings to watch are:

- words with a double *t*: *attach, attack, attempt, attend, attest, attitude, attribute, attune*, etc (see **Single and double letters in words of Latin and Greek origin**, page 157)
- inflections and derivatives with a double *t*: *betting, sitter, wettest*, etc (see **Single and double consonants in inflections and derivatives**, page 147)
- words with single or double *t*: *atom, baton, metal, petal, plateau, potassium, satin* but *battle, cattle, little, rattle, battalion, batten, buttress, mattress, tattoo*
- words in which /ts/ is spelt *tz*, *z* or *zz*: *blitz, chintz, ersatz, glitz, hertz, kibbutz, quartz, schmaltz, schnitzel, waltz*; *Nazi, scherzo, schizophrenia*; *intermezzo, mezzo-soprano, pizza*
- *posthumous* and *thyme* with /t/ represented by *th*; also *th* in names, e.g. *Anthony, Esther, Neanderthal, Thailand, Thames, Thomas*
- *eighth*, with /t-th/ spelt with one *t*
- words with a silent *b*, *c*, *ch* or *d*: *debt, doubt, subtle; indict, victuals; yacht; veldt*
- words with a silent *p*: *ptarmigan, pterodactyl, pterosaur, ptomaine; receipt*

/v/

V almost never occurs as a double letter in English, so there are fewer spelling problems than with most consonants:

avid, bevy, clever, devil, ever, hover, lavish, level, lever, novel, novice, oven, proverb, river, seven, shiver, vivid, etc

Nor does *v* usually occur as the last letter of a word:

brave, curve, delve, give, glove, have, live, love, move, sieve, solve, swerve, valve, etc

Exceptions:

- slang short forms such as *gov/guv, lav, perv, rev, spiv*
- *bovver, chivvy* (also *chivy*), *civvies, navvy, savvy, skivvy; revved, revving*

Other spellings to watch are:

- *of* and *off*
- *of* and *'ve: I should've done it,* not ✗ *I should of done it*
- *nephew* (for some people)

/w/ and /wh/

For those whose accents do not distinguish /w/ and /wh/ (e.g. *weather* and *whether, witch* and *which*), care must be taken with words spelt *wh* (though many of them are common words that cause no problems):

whack, wheeze, whelp, whether, whimper, whimsical, whiny, whippet, whirl, whisk, whisker, whisper, whittle, whizz or *whiz, whoop, whopper, whorl,* etc; *overwhelm;* also *whoa*

Other spellings to watch are:

- words with /k/ followed by /w/: *adequate, banquet, conquest, eloquent, frequent, inquest, inquiry, liquid, marquis, qualm, quarantine, quarter, quiz, quote, tranquil,* etc, but *choir, coiffure* and *cuisine;* for the *cq* spelling of *acquaint, acquire, acquit,* see page 162.
- words with /g/ followed by /w/, always spelt *gu:*

guacamole, guano, guava; anguish, languid, languish, language, sanguine, etc

- words with /s/ followed by /w/, always spelt with *su*: *assuage, dissuade, persuade, suave, suede, suite*
- words of French origin with an *oi* spelling: *boudoir, bourgeois* and *bourgeoisie, chamois, coiffeur* and *coiffure, memoir, patois, repertoire, reservoir, soiree*
- *cuisine, marijuana*

/y/

Spellings to watch are:

- words beginning with *u*: *unicorn, uniform, unify, union, unique, unison, unit, universal, uranium, urine, usage, usurp, usury, uterus, utilize, utopia*
- words beginning with *eu-*: *eulogy, eunuch, euphoria, euthanasia* (see page 220); words formed with *neuro-, pneumo-, pseudo-*
- *hallelujah* or *alleluia*

/z/

Spellings to watch are:

- words ending in *-ise* and *-ize* (see page 198)
- *blizzard, buzzard* but *hazard, lizard, wizard*
- words spelt with *s* rather than *z*: *arouse, blouse, bosom, bruise, browse, busy, cheese, choose, closet, clumsy, crimson, cruise, damson, desert, disaster, disease, flimsy, fuselage, pansy, pause, please, poise, praise, present, tease, turquoise,* etc, as opposed to *breeze, lizard,* etc
- *abysmal, aneurysm, cataclysm, chasm, cosmic, en-*

thusiasm, orgasm, paroxysm, plasma, prism, sarcasm, spasm
- common words with a double *s*: *dessert, dissolve, possess, scissors*
- words beginning with *x*: *xenophobia, Xerox, xylophone*

/zh/
Most /zh/ words are spelt with *s*: *leisure, measure, pleasure, treasure; casual, usual; derision, precision, profusion, vision,* etc.

Spellings to watch are:

- two common words spelt with *z*: *azure, seizure*
- *equation*, spelt with a *t*
- words of French origin spelt with *g*: *barrage, beige, blancmange, bourgeois, camouflage, collage, cortege, dressage, entourage, espionage, fuselage, garage* (in some pronunciations), *gigolo, largesse, lingerie, massage, ménage, mirage, negligee, prestige, protégé, regime, reportage, rouge, sabotage*

8

Spelling problems and spelling rules: word-endings

-able or -ible

The adjective endings -able and -ible (as in *eatable* and *edible*) have their origins in Latin grammar. In Latin, certain words predictably end in -abilis and others in -ibilis. These Latin word-endings have come into English as -able and -ible, but unfortunately, since English grammar is nothing like Latin grammar, the choice between -able and -ible is not as predictable in English as it is in Latin. There are, however, a number of clues and rules of thumb that will help you make the right decision.

-able

- If the 'base' or 'core' of a word ending in /əbl/ is recognizable as an English word, the ending is likely to be -able:

adapt, adaptable	break, breakable
buy, buyable	comfort, comfortable
count, countable	drink, drinkable
eat, eatable	play, playable
print, printable	

In considering what is or is not a 'recognizable English word', you must take into account some of the spelling rules mentioned in Chapters 6 and 7:

consonant-doubling (page 147):

bid, biddable	forget, forgettable
regret, regrettable	stop, unstoppable
win, winnable	

e-dropping (page 199):

adore, adorable	advise, advisable
believe, believable	debate, debatable
excuse, excusable	note, notable

y to i (page 118):

classify, classifiable	deny, undeniable
envy, enviable	rely, reliable
vary, variable	

The application of any of these rules does not prevent the core from being a 'recognizable word', and so the ending is -able in all these cases.

-able is also the spelling used when the ending is added to a phrase:

get at > ungetatable   *put down > unputdownable*

SPELLING NOTES

- A silent *e* is not dropped before *-able* if it is needed to keep *c* pronounced /s/ or *g* pronounced /j/:

enforce, enforceable	*notice, noticeable*
pronounce,	*replace, irreplaceable*
unpronounceable	
change, changeable	*manage, manageable*
knowledge,	
knowledgeable	

- If the core word ends in a consonant followed by *le*, the *e* is not dropped when *-able* is added:

handle, handleable	*settle, settleable*
whistle, whistleable	

There are some one-syllable words which do not, or may not, drop a final *e* before *-able*:

like, likeable or *likable*; *love, lovable* or *loveable*; *hire, hireable*

See page 102 for a fuller explanation.

- If an /əbl/ word belongs to a word-family in which there are words ending in *-ality*, *-ate* or *-ation*, then it will probably be spelt *-able* even if what precedes *-able* is not a word:

hospitality, hospitable	practicality, practicable
application, applicable	estimate, estimation,
	inestimable
inflammation, inflammable	navigate, navigation, navigable
placate, implacable	satiate, insatiable
separate, separation,	
inseparable	

Exception: *sensation, sensible.*

Some family connections may be less obvious:

associate, sociable	commemorate, memorable
probation, probable	transportation, portable
capacity, capable	

- If the letter before the suffix is *i*, the suffix has to be -*able*, as there are no words ending in *iible*:

  amiable, appreciable, insatiable, liable, negotiable, pliable, sociable, viable

- If there is a hard *c* /k/ or a hard *g* /g/ before the suffix, the suffix has to be -*able*:

  amicable, applicable, despicable, educable, impeccable, implacable, inexplicable, inextricable, indefatigable, navigable, practicable

-ible

Apart from the words covered in the paragraphs above, any /əbl/ word whose 'base' or 'core' is not a recognizable English word is likely to be spelt -*ible*:

audible, compatible, credible, edible, eligible, feasible, horrible, incontrovertible, incorrigible, indelible, intelligible, invincible, *irascible, legible, negligible, ostensible, plausible, possible, rep-rehensible, susceptible, tangible, terrible, visible,* etc

Exceptions:

forcible, not ✗*forceable*
fallible, which has nothing to do with the verb *fall*

However, there are also words, such as *accessible* and *digestible*, that end in *-ible* even though the core is a recognizable word (*access, digest*). For these, there is again a rule of thumb:

If the core of a *-ble* word is a recognizable English word that is also the base of a word that ends in *-ion* (not *-ation* or *-ition*, just *-ion*), then the spelling will generally be *-ible*:

compress, compression, compressible

express, expression, inexpressible

repress, repression, irrepressible

corrupt, corruption, incorruptible

contract, contraction, contractible

digest, digestion, indigestible

combust, combustion, combustible

perfect, perfection, perfectible

flex, flexion, flexible

access, accession, accessible

coerce, coercion, coercible

depress, depression, depressible

impress, impression, impressible

interrupt, interruption, interruptible

protract, protraction, protractible

suggest, suggestion, suggestible

exhaust, exhaustion, inexhaustible

The *-ion/-ible* connection can equally be seen in word-families in which there is a change in form between the verb and the noun:

admit, admission, admissible   permit, permission, permissible
transmit, transmission,
  transmissible
perceive, perception,
  imperceptible
comprehend, comprehension,
  incomprehensible
divide, division, divisible (also
  vision, visible)
submerge, submersion,
  submersible
destroy, destruction,
  indestructible
deduce, deduction, deducible   produce, production,
                                   reproducible
reduce, reduction, reducible
convert, conversion, convertible
convince, conviction,
  convincible (also invincible)

Exceptions:

- The following words end in *-ible* even though the stem is a recognizable word but is not the stem of an *-ion* noun:

  collapsible, contemptible, discernible, gullible, resistible, responsible, reversible, sensible, vendible

- Some words allow both *-able* and *-ible* endings:

collectable or *collectible*   *confusable* or *confusible*
correctable or *correctible*   *detectable* or *detectible*
ignitable or *ignitible*   *preventable* or *preventible*

- Two words have only *-able* endings:

    deflectable, predictable

-able *again*

Some words that end in *-able* are hard to classify by
any rule:

*affable, amenable, arable, culpable, equitable, formidable,
indomitable, inevitable, inexorable, inscrutable, malleable, uncon-
scionable, vulnerable*

-acy, -asy, -icy and *-isy*

Most words in this group end in *-acy*:

*accuracy, adequacy, advocacy, aristocracy, bureaucracy, celibacy,
conspiracy, delicacy, democracy, diplomacy, efficacy, fallacy,
immediacy, inaccuracy, intimacy, intricacy, legacy, legitimacy,
literacy, lunacy, magistracy, meritocracy, numeracy, obstinacy,
papacy, pharmacy, privacy, profligacy, supremacy*

Notice that many of these words are related to words
ending in *-ate* or *-crat*:

accurate, adequate, advocate, aristocrat, bureaucrat, etc

Only four common nouns end in *-asy*:

apostasy, ecstasy, fantasy (★fantastic), idiosyncrasy

Two nouns end in *-isy*:

hypocrisy, pleurisy (★*hypocritical, pleuritic*)

Two nouns end in *-icy*:

policy (★*political*), *theodicy*

ae and *i* in plural nouns

Some nouns that end in *a* in the singular have a plural form that ends in *-ae*:

algae, antennae, formulae, larvae, nebulae and *vertebrae*

Some nouns that end in *us* in the singular have a plural form that ends in *-i*:

cacti, foci, fungi, gladioli, incubi, Magi, narcissi, nuclei, radii, streptococci, styli, syllabi, termini, uteri

Alumnae is feminine; *alumni* is masculine.

Many of these nouns also have regular plural forms:

antennas, formulas, nebulas, etc
cactuses, focuses, incubuses, styluses, etc

-ance and *-ence*

Like *-able* and *-ible*, the word-endings *-ance* and *-ence* derive from Latin, and like the *a* and *i* spellings of *-able* and *-ible*, the *a* and *e* spellings are predictable in Latin but not in English.

Fortunately, as with *-able* and *-ible*, there are some helpful rules of thumb to assist you. In fact, some of the rules are very similar.

-ance
- If the 'base' or 'core' of a word ending in /əns/ is recognizable as an English word, the ending is likely to be *-ance*:

accept, acceptance   accord, accordance
acquaint, acquaintance   allow, allowance

and similarly:

annoyance, appearance, assistance, clearance, deliverance, inheritance, performance, repentance, resistance, sufferance, utterance, etc

In considering what is or is not a 'recognizable English word', you must take into account some of the spelling rules mentioned in Chapters 6 and 7:

consonant-doubling (page 147):

admit, admittance   remit, remittance
rid, riddance

e-dropping (page 99):

assure, assurance   contrive, contrivance
encumber, encumbrance   grieve, grievance
guide, guidance   hinder, hindrance
remember, remembrance

y to i (page 118):

ally, alliance   apply, appliance
defy, defiance   rely, reliance
vary, variance

The application of any of these rules does not prevent the core from being a 'recognizable word', and so the ending is *-ance* in all these cases.

   -ance is also the spelling used when the ending is added to a phrase:

come up > come-uppance

Exceptions:

precedence; excellence; coincidence; concurrence, occurrence, recurrence; acquiescence, convalescence, deliquescence, effervescence, efflorescence, fluorescence; conference, deference, difference, inference, interference, preference, reference, transference; confidence; adherence, coherence; abhorrence; emergence; dependence, transcendence; subsidence; insistence, persistence, subsistence (and *existence*); *correspondence; reverence; divergence*

★ These are all formed from recognizable English words (*precede, excel, coincide,* etc) but because of the rules of Latin grammar, word-elements such as *ced, cell, cid, curr, esc, fer, fid, her, horr, merg, pend, scend, sid, sist, spond, ver* and *verg* are likely to be followed by *-ence*, not *-ance*.
   !! Note *assistance* and *resistance*.

• If an /əns/ word belongs to a word-family in which there are words ending in *-ate* or *-ation*, then it will probably be spelt *-ance* even if what precedes *-ance* is not a recognizable English word:

deviate, deviance   *dominate, dominance*
radiate, radiance   *tolerate, tolerance*

and similarly:

luxuriance, predominance, preponderance, remonstrance, resonance, tolerance

★ Word-families can provide clues in other ways:

circumstantial, circumstance	*extravaganza, extravagance*
ignoramus, ignorance	*pugnacious, repugnant*
substantial, substance	*vigilante, vigilance*

Exception: *violate, violence.*

• If there is a hard *c* (/k/) or a hard g (/g/) before the word-ending, the ending will be *-ance*:

significance; arrogance, elegance, extravagance

-ence

• If there is a soft *c* (/s/) or a soft *g* (/j/) before the word-ending, the word-ending will be *-ence*:

beneficence, diligence, indigence, indulgence, insurgence, intelligence, intransigence, licence, negligence, resurgence, reticence

Exceptions: *allegiance, vengeance.*

• If what precedes the word-ending is not recognizable as an English word, the ending is likely to be *-ence*. For example:

abstinence, adolescence, affluence, ambience, ambivalence, antecedence, audience, belligerence, benevolence, circumference, competence, condolence, confluence, congruence, conscience, consequence, continence, convenience, corpulence, credence, decadence, diffidence, dissidence, ebullience, efflu-

ence, eloquence, eminence, equivalence, essence, evidence, excrescence, expedience, experience, flatulence, fraudulence, imminence, impertinence, impotence, impudence, inadvertence, incandescence, incidence, incipience, indolence, influence, iridescence, jurisprudence, lenience, luminescence, magnificence, malevolence, munificence, obedience, obsolescence, omnipotence, omniscience, opulence, patience, penitence, percipience, permanence, pertinence, pestilence, prescience, presence, prevalence, prominence, providence, prudence, prurience, pubescence, putrescence, quiescence, quintessence, reminiscence, residence, resilience, resplendence, reverence, salience, science, sentence, sequence, subservience, succulence, transience, truculence, turbulence, vehemence, violence, virulence

★ Notice again the presence in many of these words of key Latin word-elements such as *ced, cid, esc, fer, fic, fid, flu, ger, sci, sid, vid, vol,* etc, which are frequently followed by *-ence*.

• An *-ence* word may belong to a word-family in which the *e* is clearly pronounced in other members of the family:

consequential, consequence   *incidental, incidence*
influential, influence   *residential, residence*
ab'sent, absence   *pre'sent, presence*

-ance *again*

There are some words that end in *-ance* for which no rule can be given:

aberrance, abeyance, ambulance, appurtenance, balance, brilliance, clairvoyance, cognisance, complaisance, connivance, coun-

tenance, distance, exorbitance, exuberance, flamboyance, fragrance, happenstance, imbalance, instance, irrelevance, luminance, maintenance, nonchalance, nuisance, parlance, petulance, protuberance, provenance, recalcitrance, recognizance, reconnaissance, relevance, reluctance, repugnance, semblance, surveillance, sustenance

-ancy *and* -ency
Note the spellings of the following:

ascendancy, discrepancy, expectancy, flagrancy, hesitancy, inconstancy, malignancy, poignancy, redundancy

complacency, consistency, contingency, deficiency, despondency, efficiency, frequency, inconsistency, insufficiency, proficiency, pungency, stridency, tendency, transparency, valency

-ant *and* -ent
The adjective and noun endings -*ant* and -*ent* cause few problems, as they follow the spellings of the related nouns:

dominance, dominant	*eminence, eminent*
redundancy, redundant	*frequency, frequent*

But note the following:

dependant, descendant, pendant are nouns; *dependent, descendent, pendent* are adjectives
independent and *superintendent* are nouns or adjectives
propellant is a noun or an adjective, *propellent* is an adjective
intendant is a noun

-ary, -ery and *-ory*

Since these three endings are all pronounced /əri/ (as in *bursary, gallery, factory*), you cannot decide which is the correct spelling for any given word from its sound alone. There are, however, some rules of thumb to help you.

-ery
- If what precedes the /əri/ ending is recognizable as an English word, the ending is likely to be *-ery*:

  buffoonery, creamery, crockery, debauchery, drollery, fishery, foolery, greenery, hatchery, mockery, quackery, rockery, trickery, witchery, etc

  In considering what is or is not a 'recognizable English word', you must take into account some of the spelling rules mentioned in Chapters 6 and 7:

  consonant-doubling (page 147):

can, cannery	*distil, distillery*
shrub, shrubbery	*snob, snobbery*

  and also:

  gunnery, nunnery, robbery, tannery, thuggery

  e-dropping (page 99):

cajole, cajolery	*machine, machinery*

  and also:

  bravery, demagoguery, drapery, drudgery, finery, forgery, imagery, knavery, nursery, midwifery, perfumery, prudery,

> *raillery, refinery, savagery, scenery, slavery, vinery, winery,* etc

-ery is also the spelling used when the ending is added
to a phrase:

> *do-goodery, jiggery-pokery*

- Many *-ery* nouns are associated with a verb or noun
  ending with *-er*; for example:

> *embroider, embroidery* *flatter, flattery*
> *archer, archery*   *baker, bakery*

and also:

> *delivery, discovery, mastery, recovery, upholstery*
> *bindery, brewery, butchery, colliery, confectioner, cutlery,*
> *haberdashery, hosiery, ironmongery, jewellery, joinery, lech-*
> *ery, millinery, pottery, soldiery*

- Many *-ery* adjectives are related to verbs and nouns
  ending in *-er*:

> *bluster, blustery*   *shiver, shivery*
> *feather, feathery* *flower, flowery*

and also:

> *doddery, slithery, spluttery, tottery, wavery*
> *buttery, cindery, coppery, gingery, leathery, papery, peppery,*
> *powdery, rubbery, spidery, splintery, thundery, whiskery,*
> *watery*

Note also *slippery*.

But most /əri/ adjectives end in *-ary* or *-ory* (see
below).

- Some *-ery* words are not covered by any obvious rule:

  adultery, artery, artillery, battery, celery, cemetery, chicanery, dysentery, effrontery, frippery, gallery, livery, lottery, misery, monastery, mystery, periphery, presbytery, scullery, stationery, surgery, thievery, tomfoolery, treachery

-ary *and* -ory

Word-families may help with a few spellings; for example:

categorical, category	*directorial, directory*
historic, history	*oratorio, oratory*
victorious, victory	
arbitration, arbitrary	*contemporaneous, contemporary*
imagination, imaginary	*secretarial, secretary*
seminarian, seminary	*veterinarian, veterinary*

Meaning can sometimes be a clue:

- Nouns ending in *-ary* may refer to:

  a person in a particular job or status (*adversary, apothecary, beneficiary, dignitary, emissary, functionary, intermediary, luminary, missionary, notary, plenipotentiary, secretary*)

  a place for where something is kept or done (*apiary, aviary, dispensary, library, mortuary, penitentiary, sanctuary, seminary*)

  a collection or group (*constabulary, glossary, judiciary, justiciary, vocabulary*)

  an activity (*burglary, plagiary, topiary*)

- Other nouns ending in *-ary*:

anniversary, boundary, capillary, centenary, commentary, corollary, dictionary, dromedary, estuary, formulary, granary, itinerary, legionary, obituary, quandary, rosary, salary, summary, tributary, vagary, voluptuary

- Adjectives ending in -*ary* often denote a relationship to something:

  budgetary, cautionary, complementary, complimentary, customary, deflationary, devolutionary, dietary, disciplinary, discretionary, documentary, elementary, evolutionary, expeditionary, fragmentary, inflationary, legendary, momentary, parliamentary, planetary, precautionary, probationary, reactionary, revolutionary, rudimentary, secondary, sedimentary, supplementary, unitary, visionary

- Other adjectives ending in -*ary*:

  alimentary, ancillary, arbitrary, auxiliary, binary, contemporary, contrary, culinary, domiciliary, epistolary, exemplary, extemporary, extraordinary, funerary, hereditary, honorary, imaginary, incendiary, insanitary, involuntary, literary, mammary, mercenary, military, monetary, necessary, numerary, ordinary, pecuniary, pituitary, plenary, preliminary, primary, proprietary, pulmonary, rotary, salivary, salutary, sanguinary, sanitary, sedentary, solitary, stationary, subsidiary, supernumerary, temporary, tertiary, tutelary, voluntary

- Nouns ending in -*ory* may refer to:
     a place (*conservatory, depository, dormitory, factory, laboratory, lavatory, observatory, oratory, priory, promontory, purgatory, rectory, refectory, reformatory*)
  a person in a certain capacity (*accessory, signatory*)
- Other nouns ending in -*ory*:

allegory, category, chicory, depilatory, directory, hickory, history, inventory, memory, offertory, pillory, suppository, territory, theory, trajectory, victory

- Adjectives ending in *-ory*:

admonitory, adulatory, advisory, amatory, auditory, circulatory, conciliatory, contradictory, contributory, cursory, declamatory, defamatory, delusory, deprecatory, derisory, derogatory, desultory, dilatory, exclamatory, explanatory, exploratory, extrasensory, illusory, inflammatory, introductory, mandatory, migratory, obligatory, peremptory, perfunctory, placatory, predatory, preparatory, promissory, repertory, respiratory, revelatory, satisfactory, sensory, statutory, supervisory, transitory, valedictory

Cautionary notes:

- Do not confuse *stationary* (= 'not moving') and *stationery* (= 'paper and envelopes'); nor *summery* (= 'like summer') and *summary* (= 'short version').
- Note the spelling of *savoury* and *armoury*, related to *savour* and *armour*.

-er, -or and -ar
Nouns
-er
The most common form of the three is *-er*. You can add *-er* to almost any verb to make a 'doer' noun:

builder, deserter, grumbler, joiner, labourer, maker, painter, reader, reporter, runner, singer, speaker, teacher, walker, worker, writer

There are a few *-er* nouns formed from adjectives or nouns rather than verbs; for example:

carpenter, foreigner, idolater, jeweller, lawyer, mariner, prisoner, sorcerer, treasurer

-ar

There are only a few 'doer' nouns that end in *-ar*:

beggar, burglar, bursar, friar, liar, pedlar, registrar, scholar, vicar

There are other nouns that end in *-ar* that do not belong to the 'doer' class. In some the *a* is clearly pronounced:

caviar, cigar, guitar, hussar, jaguar, quasar, radar, seminar, sonar

In others the *a* is pronounced /ə/:

altar, calendar, caterpillar, cedar, cellar, collar, cougar, dollar, exemplar, grammar (★ grammatical), hangar, mortar, nectar, pillar, poplar, sugar, vinegar

Note also *binoculars*.

-or

We owe the *-or* spellings of these 'doer' words to Latin. Fortunately Latin also provides a few clues by which some of the *-or* spellings can be predicted.

- Many of the words end in *-ator*, *-itor* or *-utor*:

  accelerator, adjudicator, administrator, agitator, animator, arbitrator, aviator, calculator, collaborator, commentator, communicator, conspirator, creator, curator, decorator, demonstrator, detonator, dictator, duplicator, educator, elevator,

- Many nouns that end in *-tion* have corresponding adjectives in *-tious*; for example:

ambition, ambitious	*caution, cautious*
infection, infectious	*nutrition, nutritious*
ostentation, ostentatious	*superstition, superstitious*

-eous

Words ending in *-eous* can be grouped into four categories:

- Words in which the *e* belongs to the base or core word rather than to the ending itself:

advantage, advantageous	*courage, courageous*
outrage, outrageous	
nausea, nauseous	
consanguineity,	*heterogeneity, heterogeneous*
consanguineous	
homogeneity, homogeneous	

- Words that end in /-ay-ni-əs/:

  contemporaneous, extraneous, instantaneous, miscellaneous, simultaneous, spontaneous, subcutaneous

- Scientific or technical adjectives often end in *-ceous*:

  carbonaceous, cetaceous, cretaceous, herbaceous, sebaceous

  Also the non-technical word *curvaceous,* and four technical adjectives:

  aqueous, gaseous, igneous, vitreous

That leaves a small group of *-eous* words that are hard to classify in any helpful way:

beauteous, bounteous, courteous, discourteous, erroneous, gorgeous, hideous, piteous, plenteous, righteous

And *predacious* and *predaceous*, both of which are correct.

-*ise* or -*ize*

> *You must write 'advertise' but 'organize', 'improvise' but 'moralize', 'chastise' but 'cauterize'. Why? Well, it would take a long time to explain, . . .*
>
> A P Herbert, *What a Word!*

A P Herbert is in fact wrong on two counts: you don't have to write *organize, moralize* and *cauterize*; and it doesn't take very long to explain why.

Both -ise *and* -ize *correct*

Most verbs that end in /iez/ can be spelt either -*ise* or -*ize*. The rules are very simple:

* If what comes before the /iez/ ending is recognizable as an English word, then /iez/ is a word-ending and both -*ise* and -*ize* are correct:

critic, criticise or *criticize*	*equal, equalise* or *equalize*
ideal, idealise or *idealize*	*item, itemise* or *itemize*
modern, modernise or *modernize*	*moral, moralise* or *moralize*
organ, organise or *organize*	*victim, victimise* or *victimize*

In considering what is or is not a 'recognizable English word', you must take into account some of the spelling rules such as *e*-dropping (page 99):

fertile, fertilise or *fertilize*   *oxide, oxidise* or *oxidize*

In some cases, the core word is not in common use:

pulver, pulverise or *pulverize*

- In words in which the /iez/ ending could be replaced by another word-ending to form a recognizable and related English word, /iez/ is a word-ending and both *-ise* and *-ize* are correct (this is true even if what precedes the word-ending is not an English word):

  antagonist = antagon + ist: so *antagonise* and *antagonize* both correct

  harmonic = harmon(y) + ic: so *harmonise* and *harmonize* both correct

  minimal = minim(um) + al: so *minimise* and *minimize* both correct

  ostracism = ostrac + ism: so *ostracise* and *ostracize* both correct

  recognition = recogn + ition: so *recognise* and *recognize* both correct

  sympathetic = sympath(y) + etic: so *sympathise* and *sympathize* both correct

In some cases, the base form of the verb changes slightly, but the principle remains the same:

synthetic = synthet + ic: *synthesise* and *synthesize* both correct

A few words do not really fit the rules very well; for example:

cautery, cauterise and *cauterize*

The *-ize* spelling is now standard in American English and is becoming increasingly common in British English, although the -*ise* spelling is still preferred by many users of British English.

Only -ise *correct*

If neither of the above rules applies, /iez/ is part of the verb, not a suffix, and only -*ise* is correct:

advise, apprise, arise, chastise, circumcise, comprise, compromise, despise, devise, disguise, excise, exercise, franchise, improvise, incise, revise, supervise, surmise, surprise, televise

The same spelling applies when any of these words are used as nouns.

Advertise belongs to this group: *advert* is short for *advertisement*, and the -*ise* ending is not a word-ending added to *advert*.

Noun and adjective spellings to note

demise, expertise, reprise, treatise
concise, precise

Only -ize *correct*

The only correct spelling for *capsize* is with a *z*.

-yse

A few verbs are spelt -*yse*:

analyse, breathalyse, paralyse, psychoanalyse

These verbs are regularly spelt with a *z* in American English.

-ity or *-ety*
-ity
Nearly all nouns ending in /iti/ are spelt *-ity*:

ability, audacity, identity, morality, jollity, reality, sanctity

The rule of *e*-dropping (see page 99) applies:

agile, agility	*futile, futility*
grave, gravity	*immense, immensity*
scarce, scarcity	

Exceptions:
A few nouns end in *-ety*:

entire, entirety	*naive, naivety*
nice, nicety	*sure, surety*

A few nouns related to adjectives that end in *-eous* have the ending *-eity*:

heterogeneity, homogeneity, instantaneity, spontaneity

For nouns ending in *-city* and *-sity*, word-families may help:

animosity, curiosity, diversity, generosity, pomposity, verbosity, etc (★ animus, curious, diverse, generous, pompous, verbose, etc)

but:

atrocity, loquacity, mendacity, publicity, etc (★ atrocious, loquacious, mendacious, public, etc)

-ety

Several nouns, most of them related to adjectives that end in with *-ious,* have the ending *-iety*:

anxiety, dubiety, impiety, impropriety, notoriety, piety, propriety, satiety, sobriety, society, variety

Note *gay, gaiety.*

-ly

For spelling problems relating to the word-ending *-ly,* see *e-dropping* (page 99), *ll* (page 139), and *y to i* (page 118).

Adjectives ending in *-ic* add *-ally* to form adverbs:

basic, basically   *frantic, frantically*

But note *public, publicly.*

-or or *-our*

Most 'doer' nouns end in *-or*:

actor, director, survivor, etc (see page 000).

Nouns ending in *-our* tend to denote abstract nouns rather than people or things:

armour, behaviour, candour, clamour, clangour, colour, demeanour, disfavour, dishonour, endeavour, favour, fervour, flavour, glamour, harbour, honour, humour, labour, neighbour, odour, rancour, rigour, rumour, saviour, savour, splendour, succour, tumour, valour, vapour and *vigour*

In American English these words are spelt -*or*: *armor, behavior, candor*, etc. The exception is *glamour*, which is the preferred spelling in American English also, although *glamor* is correct too.

-orous

When nouns ending in -*our* form adjectives by adding -*ous*, they drop the *u*; for example:

clamour, clamorous	*glamour, glamorous*
humour, humorous	*rigour, rigorous*
valour, valorous	*vigour, vigorous*

The same happens with some other word-endings:

armour, armorial
labour, laborious
honour, honorarium, honorary, honorific
colour, coloration (but *colouration* is also correct)
glamour, glamorize (but *glamourize* is also correct)
odour, odoriferous

Before other word-endings, the *u* is not dropped:

favour, favourable	*honour, honourable*
labour, labourer	
colour, colourful	
favour, favourite	
humour, humourless	
armour, armoury	*savour, savoury*
neighbour, neighbourhood, neighbourly	

Words ending in -*ism* and -*ist* are not consistent:

behaviourism, colourist but *rigorism, humorist*

-*ous* or -*us*

The rule is simple: adjectives end in -*ous*, nouns end in -*us*.

Adjectives:

barbarous, cavernous, conspicuous, dangerous, hazardous, mountainous, poisonous, pompous, riotous, ruinous, etc

Nouns:

abacus, bonus, cactus, callus, circus, citrus, focus, foetus, fungus, ignoramus, impetus, lotus, mucus, octopus, stimulus, thesaurus, virus, etc

Exceptions:

- Adjectives that are taken directly from Latin end in -*us*:

  professor emeritus, regius professor
  pluvius insurance

- *Citrus* is both a noun and an adjective (there is also an adjective *citrous*).

Words to watch:

- nouns *fungus, mucus* and adjectives *fungous, mucous*
- *callus* (= 'hard skin'), *callous* (= 'hard-hearted')

Spelling changes:

- *e*-dropping (see page 99):

  adventure, adventurous   *desire, desirous*

  and also:

  *carnivorous, continuous, desirous, famous, fibrous, gangren-
  ous, grievous, herbivorous, nervous, omnivorous, rapturous,
  porous, rapturous, virtuous*

  In a few words an *e* is dropped before *r*:

  disaster, disastrous   *monster, monstrous*
  wonder, wondrous

  but not in:

  *adulterous, boisterous, cadaverous, cancerous, cantankerous,
  dexterous, generous, lecherous, murderous, thunderous,
  treacherous*

- *l* is doubled in *libellous* and *marvellous*, but not in
  other words:

  *credulous, frivolous, garrulous, meticulous, miraculous, peril-
  ous, querulous, ridiculous, scandalous, scrupulous, scurrilous*

-s and -es in nouns and verbs
Nouns
Plural nouns are normally formed by the addition of -*s*:

books, cats, dogs, horses, windows, years, etc

Nouns that end in *s, z, x, sh* or *ch* add -*es*:

kisses, waltzes, boxes, dishes, churches, etc

Exceptions: *quizzes, fezzes.*

The only real problems are with words that end in *o* and words that end in *y*.

o

Nouns that end in *o* mostly follow the regular rule for forming plurals and just add *-s*:

avocados, cameos, cellos, cuckoos, embryos, fiascos, hippos, kilos, kangaroos, manifestos, radios, shampoos, studios, tattoos, videos, yoyos, zoos, etc

With some nouns that end in *o*, there is a choice between adding *-s* and *-es*:

archipelagos or *archipelagoes, banjos* or *banjoes, cargos* or *cargoes, desperados* or *desperadoes, dingos* or *dingoes, dominos* or *dominoes, flamingos* or *flamingoes, ghettos* or *ghettoes, grottos* or *grottoes, halos* or *haloes, innuendos* or *innuendoes, lassos* or *lassoes, lingos* or *lingoes, mangos* or *mangoes, mementos* or *mementoes, mosquitos* or *mosquitoes, mottos* or *mottoes, porticos* or *porticoes, viragos* or *viragoes, volcanos* or *volcanoes, zeros* or *zeroes*

For poor spellers, the simplest way of handling words in this group is simply to ignore the problem altogether and treat them as if they only add *-s*; so they follow the regular rule and there is nothing special to remember.

Some nouns always add *-es* in the plural. These are the only ones that cause difficulty, because they *have to be* spelt with *-es*. Fortunately there are only a few of them:

buffaloes, echoes, embargoes, goes, heroes, Negroes, noes (*nos* and even *no's* are seen but *noes* is the one to use), *potatoes, tomatoes, tornadoes, torpedoes, vetoes*

The plural of *do* is spelt *do's*, as in *do's and don'ts*. (Note also the position of the apostrophe in *don'ts*.)

y
The rules for spellings such as *diary, diaries* and *monkey, monkeys* are covered on page 121.

French phrases
In French, adjectives have to be marked as plural if the nouns they are describing are plural. This means that if you make phrases of French origin plural in English, you may have to make more than one of the words plural; for example:

bon mot > *bons mots* not ✗ *bon mots*
bête noire > *bêtes noires* not ✗ *bête noires*
agent provocateur > *agents provocateurs* not ✗ *agent provocateurs*

In addition, the plural ending -*s* may not be where you might expect it:

raison d'être > *raisons d'être*

As a rule, you should always check the plural forms of foreign words and phrases in a dictionary.

Verbs
The regular rules for forming the third-person-singular form of verbs is much the same as for forming the plurals of nouns:

brings, crawls, fills, runs, talks, etc
misses, waltzes, fixes, washes, searches, etc

Exceptions: *quizzes.*

The only problems are again with words that end in
o and words that end in *y*.

o

The rules for verbs are not quite the same as for nouns,
but the simplest way to deal with them is to start from
the noun spellings:

- If a noun ending in *o* forms a plural by adding *-es*,
  the verb will be formed by adding *-es*:

  echoes, embargoes, goes, lassoes, torpedoes, vetoes

- If the noun adds *-s* in the plural, or if there is no
  corresponding noun, add *-s* to the verb:

  discos, memos, radios, shampoos, videos, etc

y

The rules for verb spellings such as *carry, carries* and
convey, conveys are covered at page 121.

-sion, -tion, -cion, -ction and *-xion*
-cion

To start with the simplest rule, there are only two
common words that end with *-cion*:

coercion, suspicion

Note that there are many words that end in -*cian*:

magician, musician, optician, politician, technician, etc

These words are all related to words ending in -*ic*, -*ics*, -*ical*, etc:

magic, music, optics, politics, technical, etc

-sion *and* -tion

For -*sion* and -*tion* you need to use both pronunciation and word-families as a guide.

1. An ending that is pronounced /-zhən/ will be spelt -*sion*:

abrasion, adhesion, circumcision, cohesion, collision, collusion, conclusion, confusion, contusion, corrosion, decision, delusion, derision, diffusion, dissuasion, division, effusion, elision, envision, erosion, evasion, excision, exclusion, explosion, fusion, illusion, incision, inclusion, infusion, intrusion, lesion, occasion, persuasion, precision, protrusion, provision, revision, seclusion, suffusion, supervision, television, transfusion, vision

2. If the pronunciation is /-shən/ and the ending is preceded by a *vowel*, the spelling is usually -*tion*:

addition, ambition, audition, aviation, caution, citation, creation, deletion, devotion, dilation, dilution, donation, duration, edition, elation, emotion, equation, fixation, fruition, gyration, ignition, legation, libation, location, lotion, munition, mutation, nation, negation, notation, notion, oration, ovation, petition, position, relation, rotation, sedation, sedition, solution, station, taxation, tuition, vacation, vexation, vocation, volition

3. An ending pronounced /-shən/ following a vowel may also be spelt *-ssion*. To recognize the words in this category, you need the help of word-families:

- Nouns related to verbs ending in *-cede* and *-ceed* end in *-ssion*:

  accede, accession   *concede, concession*

  and also:

  cession, intercession, precession, procession, recession, secession, succession

- Nouns related to verbs ending in *-mit* end in *-ssion*:

  admit, admission   *commit, commission*

  and also:

  emission, omission, permission, remission, submission, transmission

- Nouns related to verbs ending in *-ss* or adjectives ending in *-ssive* end in *-ssion*:

  compress, compression   *confess, confession*
  aggressive, aggression   *possessive, possession*

  and also:

  concussion, depression, digression, discussion, expression, impression, obsession, oppression, profession, progression, regression, repression, suppression, transgression

  In addition, note the following *-ssion* nouns:

  compassion, fission, mission, passion, session

4. If the ending is pronounced /-chən/, it will be spelt with a *t*:

combustion, congestion, digestion, exhaustion, indigestion, question, suggestion

5. After most consonants, the spelling is *-tion*:

absorption, action, affection, attraction, auction, benefaction, caption, collection, concoction, conjunction, connection, consumption, contraption, conviction, deception, defection, dejection, description, destruction, diction, disruption, distinction, eruption, exception, exemption, fiction, fraction, function, gumption infection, injunction, inscription, interruption, obstruction, option, perception, presumption, reaction, reception, redemption, restriction, satisfaction, section, subscription

Word-families may often help to confirm this:

affect, affection   *attract, attraction*
disrupt, disruption   *restrict, restriction*

But after *l*, the spelling is always *-sion*:

compulsion, convulsion, emulsion, expulsion, propulsion, repulsion, revulsion

After *n* the spelling is often *-sion*:

apprehension, ascension, comprehension, condescension, declension, dimension, dissension, distension, expansion, extension, introversion, mansion, pension, pretension, scansion, suspension, tension

But words belonging to certain word-families are spelt *-tion*:

attend, attention *contend, contention*
intend, intention

invent, invention *prevent, prevention*

convene, convention *intervene, intervention*

abstain, abstention *detain, detention*
retain, retention

Also notice: *mention*.

After *r* the spelling is often *-sion*:

aspersion, aversion, conversion, dispersion, diversion, excursion, extroversion, immersion, perversion, incursion, submersion, subversion, version

but on the other hand:

abortion, assertion, contortion, desertion, distortion, exertion, extortion, insertion, portion, proportion

-ction *or* -xion

Most nouns with the ending pronounced /-k-shən/ are spelt *ct*:

action, collection, conviction, deflection, distinction, erection, extinction, extraction, inflection, instruction, protection, reflection, etc

These words are based on a verb or adjective that ends in *ct*, so the word-family gives a clue to the spelling:

act, collect, convict, deflect, distinct, erect, extinct, etc

Thanks to Latin grammar, word-families help in other ways:

deduce, deductive, deduction
introduce, introductory, introduction
produce, productive, production
reduce, reduction
dissect, section (the *sect* part of these words denotes 'cutting')
satisfactory, satisfaction

In British English, but not American English, a few words may be spelt with either *ct* or *x*:

connexion, deflexion, genuflexion, inflexion, reflexion, retroflexion

but in all these cases, the preferred spelling is *ct*.
   Five words are spelt *x*:

complexion, crucifixion, flexion (also *flection*), *fluxion* and *trans-fixion*

Word-families again make the spellings clear:

complex, crucifix, flex, flux, transfix

-*x* and -*s* in plural nouns of French origin

French nouns ending in *eu* or *eau* regularly add an -*x* in the plural. In English, they may have either the French -*x* in the plural or else the normal English -*s*:

adieus or *adieux*   *beaus* or *beaux*

and similarly for:

bijou, bureau, château, gâteau, milieu, plateau, portmanteau, tableau, trousseau

y, ey or *ie* in nouns

Most English nouns that end in /i/ are spelt with a *y*:

baby, berry, body, comedy, daddy, dairy, ferry, fairy, library, lorry, melody, mummy, policy, pony, poppy, rugby, etc

Some words are spelt *ey*. Among the most common of these are:

abbey, alley, attorney, barley, chimney, Cockney, covey, donkey, galley, hockey, honey, jersey, jockey, journey, kidney, lackey, medley, money, monkey, osprey, parley, parsley, pulley, trolley, turkey, valley, volley

A few words have both *y* and *ey* spellings, e.g. *curtsy* or *curtsey, gully* or *gulley.*
   Note the following:

- A *story* is a tale. A *storey* is one floor or level of a building (but spelt *story* in American English).
- *Whisky* is the correct spelling for the drinks produced in Scotland, Wales and Canada, but *whiskey* is the spelling for the drinks produced in Ireland and the United States.

Some nouns end in *ie*. These include the following:

- some short forms, e.g. *Aussie, bookie, budgie, ciggie, commie, goalie, hankie, leftie, mountie, movie, nightie, piccie, postie, pressie* or *prezzie, trannie*
- nouns formed from adjectives, such as *baddie, biggie, brownie, daftie, dearie, freebie, goodie, meanie, oldie, quickie, sweetie* but *fatty*
- certain other nouns, such as *collie, cookie, coolie,*

> *genie, groupie, lingerie, prairie, sortie, walkie-talkie,*
> *weepie, zombie*

Diminutives and terms of endearment are generally spelt *ie*, but some may equally be spelt with a *y*:

auntie or *aunty, birdie, chappie* or *chappy, doggie* or *doggy, fishie* or *fishy, girlie* or *girly, grannie* or *granny, horsie* or *horsy/horsey, kiltie, laddie, lassie*

Some other words can be spelt *ie* or *y*:

caddie or *caddy* (in golf, but only *caddy* for keeping tea in)
ghillie, gillie or *gilly*   *hippie* or *hippy*
junkie or *junky*   *pixie* or *pixy*
rookie or *rooky*   *smoothie* or *smoothy*
softie or *softy*

Note the following: a *bogey* is a score in golf, an evil spirit or a piece of nasal mucus. A *bogie* is a low truck or part of a railway engine. A *bogy* can be any of these. (But authorities do not in fact agree on which spellings are correct for each of these meanings.)

Note that *adjectives* end in *y*:

angry, easy, fishy, funny, horsy, muddy, smoky, spicy, etc

9
Common word-forming elements

Many English words are formed, wholly or in part, from Latin and Greek word-forming elements such as the *psych* of *psychic, psychology* and *psychiatrist* and the *aqua* of *aqualung, aquarium* and *aquatic.* Learning to recognize and spell these elements can greatly improve your spelling.

In each entry, the main meaning or meanings associated with the element is given in the second column, followed by a few example words in which it occurs.

Many of these word-forming elements can be found in more than one form: for example, *derm* (relating to the skin) in *hypodermic, dermatitis* and *dermatologist.*

Also included in this chapter are other elements of Latin words that recur in many English words, such as *cid, fer, sist,* etc. Although these have no clear meaning in English words, they are worth noting as an aid to spelling.

Suffixes are dealt with in Chapter 8.

aer, aero	= air, gas	*aerate, aerobics, aerosol*
	= aircraft	*aerobatics, aerodrome, aeroplane, aeronautics*
agr, agri, agro	= farming	*agrarian, agriculture, agribusiness, agrochemical*
alg, algia	= pain	*analgesic, neuralgia, nostalgia*
ambi	= both, two	*ambidextrous, ambiguous, ambivalence*
amphi	= of both kinds	*amphibian*
	= all around	*amphitheatre*
an	= not	*analgesic, anarchism*
ann, enn	= year	*anniversary, annual, annuity, biennial, millennium, perennial*
ante	= before	*antenatal, anteroom*
anthrop, anthropo	= man, human being	*anthropoid, anthropology, misanthropist, philanthropy*
anti	= against	*anti-aircraft, antibiotic, antifreeze*
	= the opposite of	*anticlimax, anticlockwise*
aqua, aque, aqui	= water	*aqualung, aquarium, aquatic, aqueduct, aqueous, aquiculture*
arch, archy	= rule, control	*anarchy, monarch, patriarch*
	= chief	*archangel, archbishop, archipelago, architect*
archaeo	= old, ancient	*archaeology* (also in *archaic*)
astro	= star	*astronaut, astrology, astronomy, astrophysics*
aud, audio	= hearing	*audible, audience, audiovisual*

aut, auto	= done by one-self or itself	*autobiography, autograph, automatic, automobile, autonomy, autopilot*
	= relating to cars, etc	*autoroute, autosport*
bene	= good, well	*benediction, benefactor, beneficial, benefit, benevolent*
bi	= two	*bicycle, bilingual, bisect*
biblio	= book	*bibliography, bibliophile*
bio, biot	= life, living organism	*biography, biology, bioengineering, antibiotic*
bronch	= windpipe	*bronchial, bronchitis*
cardi, cardio	= heart	*cardiac, cardiograph, cardiology*
carn, carni	= flesh	*carnal, carnivorous*
cata	= bad	*catastrophe, cataclysm*
	= down	*catalogue, catalyst, catapult*

cede, ceed, sede

The most frequent spelling is *cede*:

accede, concede, intercede, precede, recede, secede

Only *supersede* has *sede*.

And for *exceed*, *proceed* and *succeed*, there is a silly (but useful) jingle:

With *ex*, *suc* and *pro*, the *e*'s together go.

ceive, ceit, cept		*conceive, deceive, perceive, receive;* *conceit, deceit, receipt;* *concept, precept;* *conception, deception, inception, perception, reception*
cent, centi	= hundred, hundredth	*centenary, centigrade, centimetre, centipede*
chrom, chromat	= colour	*chromatic, chrome, chromium, monochrome*

chron, chrono	= time	*chronic, chronicle, chronological*

cide = killing, killer

Note the following words and their meanings:

filicide (killer or killing of a child), *fratricide* (brother), *fungicide* (fungus), *genocide* (race, people), *germicide* (germs), *homicide* (human being), *herbicide* (plants), *infanticide* (child), *insecticide* (insect), *matricide* (mother), *parricide* (parent or relative), *patricide* (father), *pesticide* (insects and other pests), *regicide* (king), *sororicide* (sister), *spermicide* (sperm), *suicide* (oneself), *tyrannicide* (tyrant), *uxoricide* (wife)

circum	= round	*circumference, circumnavigate*
cise, cis		*concise, excise, incise, precise; incisive; precision*
col, com, con, cor	= with	*colleague, collect, combine, commit, accommodate, connect, consist, correlate, corrupt*
cosm, cosmo	= world, universe	*cosmic, cosmology, cosmonaut, cosmopolitan*
cracy, crat	= rule, ruler, power	*bureaucrat, democracy, aristocratic*
crypt, crypto	= hidden, secret	*cryptic, cryptogram*
cyber	= information technology, the Internet	*cybercafé, cyberspace*
cycl	= circle, wheel, rotation	*bicycle, cycle, cyclic, cyclone*
cyte, cyto	= cell	*lymphocyte, cytology*
de	= remove, make less	*declutter, decrease*
	= opposite of	*decompose, denationalize*
dec, deca	= ten	*decade, decagon*

deci	= tenth	*decilitre, decimate*
demi	= half	*demigod, demisemiquaver*
demo	= people	*democracy*
derm, dermat, dermato	= skin	*dermabrasion, hypodermic, epidermis, pachyderm, dermatitis, dermatologist*
di	= two	*dioxide, diphthong*
dia	= across, through	*diagonal, diameter, diarrhoea*
dis	= opposite of	*dissimilar*
	= undo	*disable, disconnect*
dox, doxo	= opinion, belief	*orthodox, doxology*
duce, duct		*deduce, induce, produce, reduce*
		deduct, product, etc
		deduction, induction, etc
dys	= wrong, badly	*dysfunction, dyslexic*
e	= out	*emigrate, emit*
ectomy	= surgical removal	*appendectomy, tonsillectomy, vasectomy* (compare *tomy*)
equ	= horse	*equestrianism, equitation*
equi	= equal	*equilateral, equinox*
esc, sc	= becoming (it has lost this sense in many words)	*adolescent, coalesce, convalescent, crescendo, effervescent, fluorescent, irascible, luminescence, nascent, obsolescence*
esque	= like, similar to	*picturesque, statuesque*
ethn, ethno	= race, people	*ethnic, ethnology*
eu	= good	*eulogy, euthanasia, euphoria*
extra	= outside	*extracurricular, extraordinary, extrasensory, extraterrestrial*
for	= prohibit	*forbid, forfend*
	= omit	*forbear, forget, forgo, forsake*
	= extreme	*forlorn*
fore	= front	*foreground, forearm, forename*
	= before, earlier	*forebear, forecast, foregone, foretell*

fratern, fratri	= brother	*fraternal, fraternity, fraternize, fratricide*
gam, gamy	= marriage	*bigamist, monogamous, polygamy*
gastr, gastro	= stomach	*gastritis, gastroenteritis, gastronomic*
gen	= producing	*carcinogen, genetics, hydrogen, oxygen, pathogen*
geo	= the earth	*geography, geology, geometry, geophysics*
gon	= angle	*pentagon, polygon, trigonometry*
gram	= something written, drawn or recorded	*anagram, diagram* (and *diagrammatic*), *telegram, electrocardiogram, programme, gramophone*
graph, grapho	= writing or recording instrument; record, image, writing	*electrocardiograph, tachograph, telegraph; autograph, biography, graphology, monograph, photograph*
gyn, gynaeco	= woman	*misogyny, gynaecologist*
haemo, haemato	= blood	*haematology, haemoglobin; without h in leukaemia, toxaemia, etc*
hect, hecto	= hundred	*hectare, hectolitre*
helio	= sun	*heliograph, heliotrope, helium*
hemi	= half	*hemisphere, hemidemisemiquaver*
hepta	= seven	*heptagon, heptameter*
herbi	= plant	*herbicide, herbivorous*
hetero	= other	*heterosexual, heterodox*
hexa	= six	*hexagon*
holo	= whole, complete	*holocaust, hologram*
homoeo (often **homeo**)	= similar	*homoeopathy*

homo	= same	*homophone, homosexual*
hydr, hydro	= water	*hydrant, hydroelectricity*
hyper	= over, more than normal	*hypercritical, hypersensitive, hypertext*
hypo	= under, less than normal	*hypodermic, hypothermia*
iatr	= doctor, medicine	*geriatrics, paediatrics, psychiatry*
ign, igni	= fire	*igneous, ignition*
il, im, in, ir	= not	*illegal, immodest, insane, innocent, irregular*
	= into	*immigrant, innuendo, inoculate*
infra	= below, under	*infrared, infrastructure*
inter	= between	*interactive, intercom, intermarriage, international, interrogate, interrupt, interval*
intra	= within	*intravenous*
iso	= equal	*isobar, isosceles, isotope*
itis	= inflammation	*appendicitis, arthritis, bronchitis, tonsillitis*
kilo	= thousand	*kilometre, kilowatt; kilobyte =* 1024 *bytes*
latry	= worship	*idolatry* (note spelling with single *l*)
leuco, leuk	= white blood cell	*leucocyte, leukaemia*
lith, litho	= stone	*lithography, monolithic, Neolithic*
logue	= speech	*dialogue, monologue*
	= list	*catalogue*
logy	= study, or subject studied	*archaeology, bacteriology, psychology*
	= something expressed in words	*apology, tautology, terminology, trilogy*

lysis, lyt	= decomposition, breaking up	*analysis, electrolysis, paralytic*
macro	= large, long	*macrobiotics, macroeconomics*
mal	= badly	*maladjusted, malfunction*
matern, matri	= mother	*maternity, matriarch, matricide*
mega, megalo	= large	*megalith, megalomania*
	= million	*megaton, megabyte* (= 1,000,000 or 1,048,576 bytes)
meter	= measuring device	*barometer, speedometer, thermometer*
	= distance, length	*diameter, perimeter*
metry	= measuring	*geometry, trigonometry*
micro	= small	*microbiology, microchip, microscope*
milli	= thousand, thousandth	*millimetre, millennium, millipede*
mis, miso	= hatred, hating (not the same as *mis* = badly, wrongly, as in *mislay, mislead*, etc)	*misanthropist, misogynist*
mit, miss		*commit, demit, emit, omit, permit, remit, submit* *demission, emission, omission,* etc *admittance*
mono	= one	*monogamy, monolingual, monologue, monorail, monotonous*
multi	= many	*multicoloured, multicultural, multimedia, multistorey*
naut	= sailor, sailing	*nautical, astronaut*

neo	= new, recent	*Neolithic, neo-conservative, neologism*
nephr, nephro	= kidney	*nephritis, nephrology*
neur, neuro	= nerve	*neuralgia, neuritis, neurotic*
nomy	= law	*astronomy, gastronomy*
oct, octa, octo	= eight	*octave, octagon, octopus*
oid	= like	*anthropoid, asteroid*
omni	= all, everything	*omnipotent, omniscient, omnivorous*
onym	= name; word	*pseudonym; antonym, synonym*
ophthalm, ophthalmo	= eye	*ophthalmic, ophthalmologist*
ortho	= straight, correct	*orthodontics, orthodox, orthopaedic*
osis	= illness, condition	*neurosis, psychosis, thrombosis*
	= process	*hypnosis, metamorphosis, osmosis*
osteo	= bone	*osteopath, osteoporosis*
paed, paedo	= child	*orthopaedics, paediatrics, paedophile*
palae, palaeo	= ancient, early	*Palaeolithic, Palaeozoic*
para	= beyond; subsidiary	*paranormal; paramedic*
patern, patr	= father	*paternal, patriarch, patricide*
path, patho, pathy	= illness, suffering	*psychopath, pathology*
	= feeling	*sympathy, telepathy*
penta	= five	*pentagon, pentathlon*
peri	= round	*perimeter, peripatetic, peripheral, periphrastic*
pharmac, pharmaco	= medicine, drug	*pharmaceutical, pharmacy, pharmacology*
phil, philo, phile, philia	= liking, loving	*philanthropy, philharmonic, philosophy, Francophile, Anglophilia*

phobe, phobia	= fearing, hating	*technophobe, claustrophobia, xenophobia*
phon, phone, phono	= sound, voice, speaking	*phonetic, phonic, phonology, megaphone, microphone, telephone, xylophone*
photo	= light	*photoelectric, photosynthesis*
	= photography	*photocopy*
physi, physio	= nature	*physics*
	= body	*physical, physiology, physiotherapy*
pleg, plegia	= paralysis	*paraplegic, quadraplegic, hemiplegia*
pneumat, pneumon	= air, gas, lungs	*pneumatic, pneumonia*
poly	= many	*polygamy, polygon, polytechnic*
pre	= before	*pre-war, prepare*
press		*depress, express, impress, oppress, repress, suppress*
pro	= in favour of	*pro-British*
	= forward, onward	*progress, propel*
proto	= first	*prototype, protozoa*
pseudo	= false	*pseudonym*
psych, psycho	= mind	*psychiatry, psychoanalysis, psychology*
quadr, quadri, quadru	= four	*quadrangle, quadrilateral, quadruped, quadruplet*
quasi	= to a certain extent, in appearance only	*quasi-judicial, quasi-random*
quint, quintu	= five	*quintet, quintuplet*
quire	= ask	*acquire, inquire, require*
re	= again	*redo, reprint, rewrite*
	= back	*recall, retract*
rhin, rhino	= nose	*rhinitis, rhinoceros*
rog	= ask	*interrogate, surrogate*

rrh	= flow	*catarrh, diarrhoea, haemor-rhage, haemorrhoids*
rupt	= break	*corrupt, disrupt, erupt, interrupt*
sci	= knowing	*conscience, conscientious, conscious, science, omniscient*
sect	= cut	*bisect, dissect, intersect, section*
semi	= half; almost	*semicircle, semiquaver; semifinal, semicolon, semi-precious*
sept, septu	= seven	*septet, septuplet*
sex, sextu	= six	*sextet, sextuplet*
sist		*consist, desist, insist, persist, resist* but *exist*
		consistency, insistence, persistence but *resistance*
stereo	= three-dimensional, solid	*stereophonic, stereotype*
sub, sur	= under	*submit, surrogate*
syl, sym, syn	= together with	*syllable, sympathy, syndrome, syndicate, synonym*
techn, techno	= skill, practical science	*technical, technique, technology*
tele	= distant	*telecommunications, telephone, television*
tetra	= four	*tetragonal, tetrahedron, tetravalent*
theo, the	= god	*theology, atheist, monotheistic*
therm, thermo	= heat	*thermal, thermometer, thermostat*
tomy	= surgical cutting	*lobotomy* (compare *ectomy*)
tri	= three	*triangle, tricycle, trigonometry*
ultra	= beyond	*ultrasonic, ultraviolet*
uni	= one	*unicorn, unilateral*
vor, vore	= eating, feeding on	*voracious, herbivorous, omnivorous, carnivore*

xeno	= foreign	*xenophobia*
xylo	= wood	*xylophone*
zo, zoo	= animal	*Palaeozoic, protozoa, zoology*

10
Silent letters

Silent letters are letters that are written but not pronounced. In some cases, such as the *k* of *know* and *knot* or the *w* of *wrist* and *wrong*, these letters were pronounced at an earlier stage of English, but ceased to be pronounced at some time in the past (see Chapter 2). In other cases, such as the *p* of *psychology*, the letters were pronounced in another language (in this case Greek) but are not pronounced in English. And in some cases, the silent letters are there only because scholars of the past thought they should be (sometimes quite wrongly – see page 24).

Most silent letters are not predictable. However, there are some that *are* predictable if you are aware of the word-families the words belong to. For example, the silent *g* of *sign* is predictable if you remember that *sign* is related to *signature*, in which the *g* is pronounced. Similarly, you could possibly predict the silent *g* of *phlegm* from the *g* of *phlegmatic*.

Listed below are common examples of all the silent letters.

b

debt (★*debit*), *doubt* (★*dubious*), *subtle*

aplomb, bomb, catacomb, climb, comb, coulomb, crumb, dumb, jamb, lamb, limb, numb, plumb, plumber, succumb, thumb, tomb, womb

subpoena

c

blancmange, indict, muscle (★*muscular*), *victuals*

Arctic, Antarctic

ch

fuchsia, yacht

d

grandma, handkerchief, handsome, sandwich, veldt, Wednesday, and often in *landscape*

e

- *adze, awe, axe, eye, owe.*
- *edge, hedge, judge,* etc (the *e* may be dropped, however, in *acknowledgment, judgment,* etc)
- in certain word-endings:

   active, additive, native, relative, supportive, etc
   (adjectives and nouns) *associate, deliberate, graduate, separate,* etc
   discipline, feminine, masculine, etc
   definite, favourite, opposite, etc

- after *c, s, v* and *z*:

dance, defence, fence, force, police, trance, etc
dense, corpse, else, noise, please, praise, tease, tense, these,
those, etc
give, glove, halve, have, leave, live, love, prove, shelve, sieve, etc
breeze, bronze, gauze, maize, seize, sneeze, etc

Note also:

come, some, done, none, gone, shone
minute (sixtieth part of an hour)

- breathe, clothe, loathe, sheathe, teethe and wreathe as opposed
  to breath, cloth, loath, sheath, teeth and wreath. (The /dh/
  sound is often an indication of a following silent e: seethe,
  soothe, writhe; but not in smooth or to mouth)

- gue and que, see u

ex-

Words beginning with ex- often cause problems because of
the silent c or silent h that may, or may not, come after
the x.

In most ex- words, ex is followed by a vowel. Generally, the
x is pronounced /gz/:

exacerbate, exact, exaggerate, exalt, exam, example, exasperate,
execute, exemplary, exempt, exercise, exert, exile, exist, exit,
exodus, exorbitant, exonerate, exorcise, exotic, exuberant, exude,
exult

In a few words, there is a c after the ex. In these words, the x is
pronounced /ks/, which is a clue to the presence of the c:

exceed, excel, except, excerpt, excess, excise, excite

In a few words, there is an *h* after the *ex*. In most of these words, *x* is pronounced /gz/, and in addition there is often a word-family clue to the presence of the *h*:

exhaust, exhibit (★inhibit), exhibition, exhilarate (★hilarity), exhort (★hortative), exhume (★humus)

Eccentric, ecstasy and *eczema* come from Greek, so are not formed with the Latin prefix *ex-*.

g

gnarled, gnash, gnat, gnaw, gnome, gnostic (★ agnostic), gnu

diaphragm, paradigm, phlegm (★ paradigmatic, phlegmatic)

align, assign, benign, campaign, champagne, cologne, deign, ensign, design, feign, foreign, impugn, malign, physiognomy, reign, resign, sign, sovereign (★ assignation; benignant, designation, malignant, resignation, interregnum, signature)

gh

alight, blight, bright, delight, fight, flight, fright, high, knight, light, might, nigh, night, plight, right, sigh, sight, slight, thigh, tight, wright

height, sleight

eight, freight, inveigh, neigh, neighbour, sleigh, weigh, weight

straight

aught, caught, daughter, distraught, haughty, naught, naughty, taught

bought, brought, fought, nought, ought, sought, thought

bough, doughty, drought, plough

dough, though

through

borough (but *burgh* in Scotland), *thorough*

h

heir, heiress, honest, honour, hour

aghast, dinghy, ghastly, gherkin, ghetto, ghost, ghoul, spaghetti, yoghurt

antirrhinum, catarrh, diarrhoea, haemorrhage, haemorrhoids (see page 226); also *myrrh*

rhapsody, rhea, rhesus, rhetoric, rheumatism, rhino, rhizome, rhododendron, rhombus, rhubarb, rhyme, rhythm

exhibit, exhilarate, etc (see *ex-* above)

cheetah, hallelujah, hookah, hurrah, loofah, maharajah, messiah, pariah, rajah, savannah, shah, verandah (also spelt *veranda*)

annihilate, dahlia, dhow, Fahrenheit, forehead (for many speakers), *gymkhana, jodhpurs, khaki, philharmonic* (★*harmony*), *saccharine, shepherd* (★*herd*), *silhouette, vehement, vehicle* (★*vehicular*), *zucchini*

k

knack, knapsack, knave, knead, knee, kneel, knell, knickers, knife, knight, knit, knob, knock, knot, know, knowledge, knuckle

blackguard

l

chalk, stalk, talk, walk

folk, yolk

almond, almoner, alms, balm, balmy, calm, napalm, palm, psalm, qualm, salmon

behalf, calf, half, calve, halve

should, would, could

m

mnemonic

n

autumn, column, condemn, damn, hymn, solemn (★ *autumnal, columnist, condemnation, damnation, hymnal, solemnity*)

government (★ *govern*)

p

pneumatic, pneumonia

psalm, psalter, pseudo, psittacosis, psoriasis, psychic, psychology

ptarmigan, pterodactyl, pterosaur, ptomaine

receipt

cupboard, raspberry, sapphire

French words: *corps, coup*

r

French words: *dossier, foyer, laisser-faire*

s

aisle, island, isle, islet, viscount

French words: *apropos, bourgeois, chamois, chassis, corps, debris, fracas, precis, rendezvous*

t

apostle, bristle, bustle, castle, epistle, gristle, hustle, jostle, mistletoe, nestle, pestle, rustle, thistle, trestle, whistle, wrestle

chasten, christen, fasten, glisten, listen, moisten (★ *chaste, Christ, fast,* etc); *Christmas*

often, soften (★ *oft* and *soft*)

French words ending in *et*: *ballet, beret, bouquet, buffet, cabaret, chalet, crochet, croquet, depot, duvet, gourmet, parquet, ricochet, sachet, tourniquet, valet*

other words from French: *coup d'état, debut, mortgage, pot-pourri, rapport*

boatswain (★*boat*), *waistcoat* (★*waist*)

th

asthma, isthmus

u

build, buoy, buy

guarantee, guard, guardian, guerrilla, guess, guest, guide, guild, guile, guillemot, guillotine, guilt, guinea, guise, guitar, guy catalogue, colleague, dialogue, epilogue, fatigue, fugue, intrigue, league, monologue, plague, prologue, rogue, synagogue, vague, vogue

harangue, meringue, tongue

languor (★*languid*), *Portuguese*

antique, baroque, boutique, brusque, cheque, clique, critique, mosque, mosquito, mystique, oblique, opaque, physique, pique, plaque, risqué, technique, unique

burlesque, grotesque, statuesque

conquer, quay, queue

W
wrack, wraith, wrangle, wrap, wrath, wreak, wreath, wreck, wren, wrench, wrest, wrestle, wretched, wriggle, wright, wring, wrinkle, wrist, writ, write, writhe, wrong, wrought, wry (and *awry*)

who, whom, whose; whole, whore; whooper swan, whooping cough

answer (★*swear*)*, boatswain* and *coxswain* (★*swain*)*, sword, two* (★ *twin* and *twice*)

Z
words from French: *laissez-faire, pince-nez, rendezvous*

11
Capital letters

The basic rules for using capital letters are quite straightforward: sentences begin with capital letters; and names and titles begin with capital letters.

Sentences

A sentence must begin with a capital letter:

The girl took some keys out of her bag.
We hated the cook's soggy pastry.
What are you doing?
My goodness! What a surprise!

The same is true for parts of sentences acting as if they were whole sentences:

Would the owner set off the burglar alarm? Phone the police? Chase after us with an axe?
Where does that leave the children? Or their teachers? Or the parents?

Direct speech

Sentences quoted in direct speech begin with a capital letter:

She said quietly, 'He's left me.'

If the sentence is split, the second part does not begin with a capital:

'You both know,' she said, 'what you have to do.'

Quotations

If a quotation is a complete sentence, it should begin with a capital letter:

As George Mikes once said, 'An Englishman, even if he is alone, forms an orderly queue of one.'

If the quotation is integrated into your sentence, no capital letter is needed (although some authorities prefer a capital letter):

Drummond states that 'the rise of Mitanni brought renewed crisis to the Hittite kingdom, with a number of principalities asserting their independence'.

If the quotation is not itself a complete sentence, there should be no capital letter in any case:

George Mikes once said that an Englishman, even if he is alone, 'forms an orderly queue of one'.

Poetry

In traditional poetry, each line begins with a capital letter whether or not it is the beginning of a sentence:

> *There was no leaf upon the forest bare,*
> *   No flower upon the ground,*
> *And little motion in the air*
> *   Except the mill-wheel's sound.*

Percy Bysshe Shelley, 'Archy's Song'

In modern poetry, this may not be the case. There may not even be capital letters marking the beginnings of grammatically separate sentences:

> *I said to her*
> *do not go*
> *you'll only be trapped*
> *and bewitched*
> *and will suffer in vain.*

Miroslav Holub, 'The Cat'

Names

Capitals are required for the first letter of names. Any person or thing with a unique name requires the first letter of that name, or of all the main words of the name, to be a capital; for example:

- people, gods, animals, etc:

Peter	*Lucy*	*Tony Blair*
God	*Odin*	*Ptah*
Red Rum	*Bugs Bunny*	

adjectives derived from names:

Edwardian   *Kafkaesque*   *Shakespearian*
Benedictine   *Franciscan*

and other words derived from names:

Thatcherism   *Blairite*   *Britneyfication*

- ethnic groups:

Picts   *Sioux*   *Xhosa*
Black Americans *Native Americans*

and related adjectives:

Pictish   *Siouan*

- places:

Paris   *England*   *Cornwall*
Barnton Road   *Waterloo Station* *Loch Lomond*
Mount Everest

- languages:

Italian   *Welsh*   *Esperanto*

related adjectives and nouns:

American   *French*   *Glaswegian*

and other derived words:

Americanize   *Frenchify*

- days of the week and months of the year:

Monday   *April*

- festivals:

Christmas	*Easter*	*Wesak*
Diwali	*Hanukkah*	*May Day*

- religions:

Buddhism	*Christianity*	*Islam*
Hinduism	*Sikhism*	*Roman Catholicism*

and related nouns and adjectives:

Buddhist	*Christian*	*Muslim*
Sikh	*Hindu*	*Catholic*

- organizations:

British Aerospace	*Oxford University Press*

- periods and events of history:

the Ice Age	*the Renaissance*
the Russian Revolution	

- acts of parliament, etc:

the Corn Laws	*the Declaration of Independence*

Minor words
Notice that in all the above categories, minor words such as *the* and *of* are not capitalized:

Winnie the Pooh	*Vlad the Impaler*
the Bay of Biscay	*the River Thames*
the Sea of Azov	*the Pyrenees*
Newcastle upon Tyne	*Carlton-on-Trent*

Ashford in the Water   *Weston-super-Mare*

the Church of Scotland   *the National Union of*
                                 Journalists

Action on Smoking and Health

However, in names that specifically include 'the' as part of the name, 'the' may correctly be written with a capital *T* even in the middle of a sentence:

These kids find The Salvation Army is ready to accept them.
They have an office in The Hague.

However, if the name of a newspaper or magazine is already highlighted within the sentence, it is correct to leave the word 'the' unhighlighted and not capitalize it:

✓ *He wrote a letter to The Times but it wasn't published.*
✓ *He wrote a letter to the* Times *but it wasn't published.*

In personal names of foreign origin, minor words such as *de* and *von* or *van* are usually not capitalized, but usage varies and you must simply spell names the way the people themselves spell or spelt them:

the Venus de Milo   *the Marquis de Sade*
Walter de la Mare   *Daphne Du Maurier*
Leonardo da Vinci

Baron von Richthofen

Ludwig van Beethoven   *Vincent van Gogh*
Martin Van Buren   *Sir Anthony Van Dyck*

In names beginning with *Mac* and *Mc*, the following letter may be a capital letter, or it may not:

MacDonald   *McEnroe*
Macleod   *Mackenzie*

Here again you must simply spell names the way the people themselves spell or spelt them.

In Irish names, *O* is always capitalized, and followed by a capital:

O'Brien   *O'Neill*

Words derived from names

Many words which are in origin people's names or which are derived from names, but which have lost their close association with the people concerned, do not take a capital letter:

wellingtons (named after the Duke of Wellington)
sandwich (named after the Earl of Sandwich)
watt (named after James Watt)
ampere (named after Louis Ampère)
pasteurize (from Louis Pasteur)
bowdlerize (from Thomas Bowdler)
boycott (from Charles Boycott)

Both *Platonic love* and *platonic love* are correct.

Similarly, while one may write *Bible, Gospel* and *Scripture,* it is usual to write *biblical, gospel* (as an adjective) and *scriptural.*

Personification

When abstract nouns are treated as people, for example in poetry, they are given capital letters:

When Love with unconfined wings
  Hovers within my gates . . .

Richard Lovelace, 'To Althea from Prison'

I love waves, and winds, and storms,
  Everything almost
Which is Nature's, . . .

Percy Bysshe Shelley, 'Invocation'

Brand names

Strictly speaking, capital letters are required with all proprietary names: *Hoover, Xerox,* etc. When words like these come to be used as general terms for the objects they denote and the activities they are used for, without implying the use of products of particular companies, they are usually written without capitals: *hoover, xerox.*

Companies strongly deprecate the use of their trademarks and brand names as generic terms written without capital letters, as this threatens their trademark status. So although it is acceptable, indeed perfectly normal, not to use capitals for words like *hoover* in informal writing, you should in formal and technical writing be careful to use a capital letter with any word that is a trademark or brand name. Check in your dictionary: all such words should be marked with an ® or some other indicator of their proprietary status.

The capital is optional when any of these words are used as verbs.

Planets

Planet and star names are written with capital letters:

Jupiter   *Mars*   *Alpha Centauri*

However, *Earth* may be written *earth* where it is clear that it is the planet that is being referred to, not 'soil' or 'ground'. The same applies to the *Moon*.

In idioms, do not use capitals:

What on earth are you doing?
He was over the moon about it.

Countries, regions and towns

Names of countries and regions require capital letters:

the Middle East   *South Africa*

But a word that is not actually part of the name of a definite place does not require a capital letter:

central London   *southern Africa*

Therefore it is correct to write

the Republic of South Africa (the name of the country)

but:

South Africa is a republic.

Similarly:

They live in the south of France.

But:

They live in the South. ('the South' being understood as a definite area)

Words denoting places of origin

Words relating to places are written with capital letters:

German sausages   *French wines*

This is true even if the words no longer imply a real relationship with a place:

Danish pastries   *French windows*
Brussels sprouts   *Cheddar cheese*
Cornish pasties   *Dutch courage*

Some people write *danish pastries, french windows,* etc, but most authorities prefer the capital letters.

Both *plaster of Paris* and *plaster of paris* are correct.

Titles

Words that are used in titles should begin with capital letters:

the Archbishop of Canterbury   *the Prime Minister*
the President of the United   *Queen Mary*
  States
Sir Bernard Lyons   *Baroness Thatcher*
the Prophet Muhammad   *the Three Musketeers*
Parliament   *the Government*

The same words do not, of course, require capitals when they are not being used in titles:

How many prime ministers have there been since Disraeli?
There have been two English queens with the name of Elizabeth.
Scotland has its own parliament.
Saint Jude is the patron saint of hopeless causes.
He knows a lot about Norse gods and goddesses.

When a title is hyphenated, both parts should have capital letters:

Major-General Gordon

Titles of books, plays, etc

All the main words (the nouns, pronouns, verbs, adjectives and adverbs) in the title of a book, play, film, etc must begin with a capital letter, whereas the minor words (the articles *the* and *a/an*, prepositions and conjunctions) should not have capitals. Nonetheless, the first and last words in a title must always begin with a capital letter:

I'm looking for a book called 'The Men and the Girls'.
You really must read 'Freedom in a Rocking Boat'.
Who sang 'It's My Party and I'll Cry if I Want To'?

If there is a hyphenated compound in a title, both parts are usually written with initial capital letters:

Have you got a copy of 'Managing the Non-Profit Organization'?

There is a more recent school of thought, especially in academic circles, that prefers only the first words in book titles, etc to have capitals:

One of your set books for this term is 'Freedom in a rocking boat'.

Unless you are specifically required to follow this practice, you should keep to the traditional style with capitals for all the important words.

Seasons

The names of seasons are not usually written with capital letters (thus: *winter, summer, autumn*), but it is correct to write *Spring* if necessary for the sake of clarity.

Subjects of study

Subjects of study are not normally written with initial capital letters:

We've got two periods of maths this morning, then two periods of chemistry.

However, the name of the subject may require a capital letter on other grounds:

Have we got French today?

However, when a subject of study is part of the title of a course, degree, etc, it should be written with a capital letter:

She's got a BSc in Physics and the Philosophy of Science.

Abbreviations and symbols

Abbreviations that consist of the initial letters of two or more words are usually written completely in capital letters:

AGM, APR (= 'annual percentage rate'), *BA, BBC, MOT, NUM, PLC, PS* (= 'postscript'), *TLC* (= 'tender loving care'), *USA, WSW* (= 'west-south-west'), etc

When an abbreviation takes in more than the first letter of a word, only the first letter is a capital:

BSc (= 'Bachelor of Science'), *PhD* or *DPhil* (= 'Doctor of Philosophy')

The abbreviations of the names of some organizations, etc have become established as names and are pronounced as single words. In such cases, the names may be spelt entirely in capital letters or with only an initial capital:

NATO or *Nato, UNESCO* or *Unesco, AIDS* or *Aids,* etc

Some abbreviations of this type are now so well established in the language that they are never written with capital letters:

radar (= 'radio detection and ranging')
sonar (= 'sound navigation and ranging')

In the abbreviated forms of the names of some organizations that have 'of' or 'for' in their name, the 'of' and 'for' may be abbreviated to a capital letter or a lower-case letter. In such cases, follow the practice of the organization concerned:

FoE or *FOE* (= 'Friends of the Earth')
DfES (= 'Department for Education and Skills')
DFID (= 'Department for International Development')

A few abbreviations may be written with lower-case letters:

AGM or *agm, AKA* or *aka* (= 'also known as'), *BCG* or *bcg,* *PLC* or *plc*

Some abbreviations are always (or nearly always) written with lower-case letters:

asap (= 'as soon as possible'), *fob* (= 'free on board'), *gbh* (= 'grievous bodily harm')

Abbreviations of Latin words are written in lower-case letters:

a.m., p.m., e.g., i.e., viz.

If possible, *AD* and *BC* should be written with small capitals:

Caesar invaded Britain in 55 BC.

Symbols and abbreviations for weights and measures are written in lower-case letters:

in., cm, mph, etc

The first (or only letter) of the symbol for a chemical element is written as a capital letter:

Common salt is sodium chloride, NaCl. Water is H_2O.

Post codes are written with capital letters, as are American zip (or ZIP) codes:

Edinburgh EH14 6JJ
South Dakota SD 57301

Other uses of capital letters

'Topping and tailing' letters

You write *Dear Sir, My dear Frances,* etc at the start of a letter, and at the end you write *Yours sincerely* or *Yours faithfully*.

Emphasis

Capital letters are often used for emphasis:

> *Since I have given you all this advice, I add this crowning*
> *precept, the most valuable of all: NEVER TAKE ANY-*
> *BODY'S ADVICE.*
>
> George Bernard Shaw, 'Advice to a Young Critic'

The use of capital letters for emphasis is acceptable in informal writing, but in formal writing this is better done with italics (and done sparingly).

A similar use of capitals for emphasis may sometimes be seen in adverts and headlines:

Probably the Biggest Manufacturer of Quality Sheds in Scotland

Now I Can Play a Bigger Part in My Kids' Education – Thanks
  to Home-Ed Books

Radical Cleric to Face UK Terror Charges

A humorous use of capitals for emphasis in informal writing can be seen in the following examples:

> *James I slobbered at the mouth and had favourites; he*
> *was thus a Bad King.*
>
> W C Sellar and R J Yeatman, *1066 and All That*

> *Owl hasn't exactly got Brain, but he Knows Things.*
>
> A A Milne, *Winnie-the-Pooh*

German nouns

In German, all nouns are written with capital letters. When these words are borrowed into English, they are generally still written with capital letters:

Gastarbeiter, Lebensraum, Schadenfreude, Weltanschauung, Weltschmerz

However, as such words become absorbed into English, they tend to lose their capitals; thus:

blitzkrieg, festschrift, kitsch, lederhosen, leitmotiv, lieder, realpolitik, sauerkraut, wunderkind

There is no clear ruling about which German nouns fall into which category, and authorities differ. Follow your own dictionary.

Summary of key points

- Sentences begin with capital letters.
- Quotations only require capital letters if they are complete sentences and are noteworthy in some way.
- Names and titles require capital letters. But the names of common objects and activities named after people do not need capitals.
- The first words and all the main words of the title of a book, film, play, etc should begin with capital letters.
- Many abbreviations and symbols are written with capital letters, but not the symbols for units of measurement.
- German nouns used in English may or may not be written with capital letters.

12
Hyphens

One must regard the hyphen as a blemish to be avoided wherever possible.

Attributed to Sir Winston Churchill

If this actually was Churchill's opinion, he would be a happy man today. Hyphens are employed much less frequently than they used to be. In fact, it has been estimated that there are only about half as many hyphens in written English as there were even ten years ago. To take just one example, compound nouns that were formerly hyphenated (e.g. *tea-bag*) are now generally written either as two words (*tea bag*) or as single words (*teabag*). Hyphens are much less used in American English than in British English, but British English is catching up fast.

Nevertheless, the hyphen is by no means a 'blemish to be avoided'. Correctly used, hyphens add clarity to writing by showing in black and white what stress and intonation would indicate in speech. Consider this sentence from a news report:

Thousands of illegal migrants make the perilous voyage each year,
often in rickety ships run by people smuggling rings.

Why, one might ask, do people who are smuggling
rings take illegal immigrants along as well? It must
increase the likelihood of getting caught. A hyphen
between *people* and *smuggling* would, of course, make
it clear that what is meant is that the immigrants are
in the hands of gangs of people-smugglers.

What a hyphen in *people-smuggling* would do is
show that these two words are acting as a unit in the
sentence. That is the main function of hyphens: they
link two or more words (or in some cases, parts of
words) that have to be understood as single elements
in sentences.

Phrases of two or more words

When two or more words together form a phrase that
describes a following noun, they must be hyphenated:

A village on the east coast is an east-coast village.
The people who live next door are your next-door neighbours.
Instructions that are easy to follow are easy-to-follow instructions.

Notice that such phrases require hyphens only when
they precede the noun they are describing, and not
elsewhere. Further examples are:

a twice-weekly drama series	*a no-risk, money-back guarantee*
a sixteenth-century church	*deep-sea diving*
hassle-free travel	*a not-so-tidy garden*

a dress with three-quarter-length sleeves
the soon-to-be-huge darlings of the media, Franz Ferdinand
Glits is an Edinburgh-based, female-voice choir.
Our Do-It-for-You Service is safer than DIY.
Apply for a low-cost personal loan today.
Our fertilizer lasts twice as long as off-the-shelf products.
She wasn't really a bottling-things-up sort of a person.
This was noses-pressed-against-the-window journalism.

Exception: place-names that are not normally hyphenated remain unhyphenated:

a Rio de Janeiro night club
*The Hong Kong-born businessman Alan Yau is a formidable force
  in the food industry.*
*She will tie the knot with her Los Angeles-based fiancé on
  Saturday.*

Phrases consisting of an adverb and an adjective or participle

A descriptive phrase consisting of an adverb and an adjective is not normally hyphenated:

a quite ridiculous suggestion
a very silly boy
a beautifully illustrated book
a lightly boiled egg
Place the teabag in a cup of freshly boiled water.

However, if an adverb ending in *-ly* is felt to be particularly closely linked to the following adjective (especially a past participle), it is considered acceptable by many

people to have a hyphen between the two words, as in
the following examples:

a closely-written sheet of paper
the problems of mentally-handicapped children
within easily-defined genre boundaries
picturesquely-clad gypsies
a legally-binding agreement

While permissible, this should only be done if there
really is a particular need for it, and there rarely is. As
a general rule, do not hyphenate an adverb and a
following adjective.

If any of the adverbs *well, better, best, ill, worse,
worst, much, little, most* and *least* plus a past participle
form a phrase describing a following noun, then a
hyphen is required between them:

He became one of Britain's best-loved comedy actors.
They're very well-brought-up little girls.
This is one of Hollywood's worst-kept secrets.
The tale of the ill-fated liner 'Arctic' was a sad one indeed.
Fox-hunting is a much-abused sport.
Zen calligraphy has remained a little-understood art form.
This was one of the BBC's most-watched plays.
He must be one Britain's least-trusted politicians at the moment.

No hyphen is needed when the phrase does not
immediately precede a noun:

*Although the book was well received, it took time for it to become
  as popular as it is today.*
*He is a professor of medical law, but better known to most people
  as a writer.*

She is best known and most respected for her stand against the Iraq war.
Like every other member of the family, the house is much loved.

However, compounds formed with *ill* do tend to be hyphenated even after a verb:

In my opinion, the plan was ill-conceived.
The expedition was ill-omened right from the start.

With a present participle, the tendency is to hyphenate in all positions:

She wrote a well-meaning but rather ill-informed article on unmarried motherhood.
Her suggestion was very well-meaning, I'm sure.

The same can be seen in similar constructions with other short adverbs:

The problems seem never-ending.
The study was wide-ranging and comprehensive.
My girlfriend was very long-suffering and tolerant.
The book's popularity among the public was slow-burning.
The afternoon storm was fast-moving.

Multi-word phrases functioning as nouns

Multi-word phrases acting as nouns are generally hyphenated:

my brother-in-law   *a man-about-town*
a jack-of-all-trades   *a jack-in-the-box*
forget-me-nots   *Johnny-come-latelys*

However, if the phrase is of the form 'X of Y' or 'X of the Y', there are no hyphens:

a Justice of the Peace *a guard of honour*
a man of the world   *a matron of honour*
a man of action

Exceptions: compounds with special or figurative meanings are usually hyphenated:

A Portuguese man-of-war is a sort of jellyfish.

Phrases with an added suffix

When two or more words are made to function as a single element in a sentence by the addition of a suffix (such as *-ness*), the whole compound must be hyphenated:

> *Esmond was being very Justice-of-the-Peace-y.*

> *The aunts raised their eyebrows with a good deal of To-what-are-we-indebted-for-the-honour-of-this-visitness . . .*

both examples from P G Wodehouse

Other two-word phrases

Certain other two-word phrases need hyphens:

* Numbers from 21 to 99 and fractions should always be hyphenated:

> *There were forty-three of them.*
> *Four-fifths of the population live below the official poverty line.*

- A two-word phrase in which the second element is a past or present participle or a word ending in *-ed* should always be linked by a hyphen:

  home-made   *short-staffed*
  mind-blowing   *heart-warming*

  However, some well-established compounds may be written as single words:

  heartbreaking   *heartbroken*
  crestfallen

- A combination of an adjective and a noun should be hyphenated:

  The food in the restaurant was first-rate.
  The choice of music seemed rather second-rate to me.
  The job will be pretty low-level for the foreseeable future.

- Combinations of a noun plus an adjective are hyphenated before nouns but need not be elsewhere in a sentence:

  We were wading through knee-deep mud.
  Shoulder-length hair is okay by me.
  It was a pitch-black night.

  But:

  The mud was knee deep (or knee-deep).
  Knee deep (or Knee-deep) in mud, we were making very slow progress.
  Her hair was shoulder length (or shoulder-length) and curly.
  Outside it was pitch black (or pitch-black).

Compound nouns formed with two elements

In general, a compound noun is written as two separate words if it is felt that the first word simply describes the second word, but as a hyphenated word or as a single word if the compound is felt to be a single lexical unit describing a particular category of person or thing:

a bus company   *a bus-driver*
the trade balance   *a trademark*

A compound in which the first element is the object of the second element is generally hyphenated:

bus-driver, fox-hunting, etc

or written as a single word:

hillwalking, moneylender, etc

If the 'single lexical unit' type of word is well established and in frequent use, and if it is constructed from short words, it is likely to be written without a hyphen:

bedroom, bluebottle, goldfish, teacup, tablespoon, etc

A hyphen is more likely in longer words, though many compounds that were formerly likely to be written with a hyphen are now usually written without one:

dining room, food poisoning, etc

A hyphen is also frequently used to avoid an undesirable or potentially confusing juxtaposition of letters:

heart-throb rather than *heartthrob*
time-exposure rather than *timeexposure*

All in all, the rules for this category of words are by no means fixed, and different authorities will have different preferences. When in doubt, follow the recommendations of your own dictionary.

Phrasal verbs

Phrasal verbs are combinations of simple verbs such as *get, give, put, send* or *take* with adverbs such as *in, out* or *off* or prepositions such as *for* or *with*, or both; for example:

get back, give off, knock down, pick off, put up with, warm up

Phrasal verbs should not be hyphenated:

✓ *Volunteers clean up the town.*
✓ *This event has sold out every year.*
✓ *Always allow yourself five minutes to warm up.*
✗ *Volunteers clean-up the town.*
✗ *This event has sold-out every year.*
✗ *Always allow yourself five minutes to warm-up.*
✗ *The Defence Secretary is due to make a statement on proposals to move British troops towards Baghdad to free-up US troops.*

Nouns formed from phrasal verbs

Nouns formed from phrasal verbs are often hyphenated:

Major clean-ups have been carried out thanks to the efforts of local residents.
The concert was a sell-out.
Allow yourself a five-minute warm-up.

Similarly:

fly-past, line-up, share-out, send-up, set-to, set-up, write-off, etc

In some compounds the hyphen is optional (*takeaway* or *take-away, takeover* or *take-over*) and many well-established compounds are now usually written as single words:

fallout, getaway, giveaway, hangover, layabout, layout, hideout, knockout, lookout, setback, stowaway, etc

If the verb part of the compound has a word-ending added to it, the compound is always hyphenated:

a grown-up, a passer-by, a hanger-on, etc
I'll need to give the house a good going-over.
I can't stand all this showing-off.

Adjectives formed from phrasal verbs

Adjectives formed from phrasal verbs are hyphenated when they precede a noun:

an unhoped-for success
her longed-for children
a sawn-off shotgun
a dreadfully hung-up young man
knock-down prices

In other positions, the rules are more fluid. Current usage seems to prefer to leave combinations of verbs and prepositions (such as *for, of* or *with*) hyphenated, but combinations of verbs and adverbs (such as *by, in, out, past* or *up*) unhyphenated; thus:

His success was quite unexpected, indeed unhoped-for.
He was really hung up about what had happened.

But when the phrase is not felt to be acting as an adjective, no hyphen is needed:

Children had been longed for and tried for for many years.

Hyphens with prefixes, suffixes and other word-forming elements

In general, hyphens are not used with prefixes (*un-*, *dis-*, *mis-*, *pre-*, *re-*, etc), suffixes (*-ly*, *-ness*, *-ful*, *-dom*, etc) or word-forming elements (*electro-*, *hydro-*, *photo-*, *-itis*, *-lysis*, etc).

But a hyphen is correctly used:

- to avoid the juxtaposition of identical letters, especially vowels (e.g. *re-enter*, *pre-eclampsia*, *electro-optics*, *anti-inflammatory*)
- to distinguish words that would otherwise be identical (*re-cover* = 'cover again', and *recover* = 'get better', *re-count* = 'count again' and *recount* = 'tell', *co-op* and *coop*)
- to clarify the structure of uncommon words that might not at first sight be understood:

    Many of the animals in the abattoir had been mis-stunned.

Prefixes

- If *un-* is added to a word beginning with a capital letter, the new word is usually hyphenated: *un-American*, *un-Islamic*, etc. But it is now acceptable, though much less common, to write such words without hyphens: *unChristian,* etc.

- *ex-, non-* and *pro-* are usually followed by hyphens: *ex-wife, non-flammable, pro-life.*

  Exceptions: *nonconformist, nondescript, nonentity, nonplus, nonsense.*

- When *ex-* precedes two or more words that form a single unit of meaning in a sentence, it should be linked to the first word with a hyphen, but the other words remain unhyphenated:

  an ex-Los Angeles policeman
  the ex-Bay City Rollers drummer

  However, if linking *ex-* to the following word produces something awkward or potentially confusing, rephrase the sentence (for example using 'former' instead of *ex-*):

  ✗ *an ex-public toilet* (is this now a private toilet?)
  ✓ *a former public toilet*

- Long-established words beginning with *co-* are now usually not hyphenated: *coefficient, cooperate, coordinate,* etc. Newer coinages, on the other hand, are likely to be hyphenated: *co-agent, co-author, co-chair, co-driver, co-educational,* etc.

  To avoid confusion, write *co-op* and *co-opt* rather than *coop* and *coopt,* but *coed* is correct.

Suffixes

Suffixes are generally not preceded by hyphens. However, for clarity it may occasionally be better to have a hyphen:

This is sheer pie-in-the-sky-ism.
He greeted him in a hail-fellow-well-met-ish sort of way.
She was Botoxed or Botox-ed to the eyeballs.
We have always fetishised or fetish-ised female bodies.
She waved a cigarette-ed hand towards the baby.

Word-forming elements

- *Anti-* is not normally followed by a hyphen: *anti-clockwise, antifreeze,* etc. But some words are hyphenated: *anti-hero, anti-marketeer,* etc. When in doubt, follow the spelling in your dictionary.

- *-itis* is often used facetiously to designate supposed diseases. Usually no hyphen is needed, but there may be one following a vowel:

  Arnie has footballitis, a disease that afflicts millions of men.
  Email is the best way to contact me as I have phone-itis.

Miscellaneous points

- Strictly speaking, *mid-* is a word-forming element like *anti-* or *contra-*. It should therefore be linked to the following word with a hyphen:

  This started in the mid-1970s.
  Two English Songs of the mid-15th century
  From mid-May to mid-June, the Mozarts stayed in Naples.
  I am in the mid-course of my life.
  By mid-afternoon many people were evidently hungry.

There is a trend nowadays towards treating *mid* as a word in its own right with omission of the hyphen:

Imported cloth became more difficult to obtain from the mid 1980s.

The record stopped in mid tune.

At present, however, hyphenated forms are still preferable, with certain exceptions:

When *mid* occurs parallel to another word that does not require a hyphen, the hyphen is best omitted:

Carrie is in her mid to late twenties.

This went on through the late third and mid to late fourth centuries AD.

Terrorist attacks increased by over 20 per cent between mid July and early August.

In some cases, e.g. certain place-names, a hyphen is not correct:

He had travelled there from his home in Mid Glamorgan.

Words formed with *self-* are hyphenated unless the second element is a suffix:

self-control, self-help but *selfless*

Compounds formed with *half-* are usually hyphenated:

half-baked, half-term, etc but *halfway, halfwit, halfpenny*

Words formed with *like* are usually hyphenated unless they are well established:

grass-like, ostrich-like but *childlike, ladylike*

- For comments on the non-hyphenation of *no one*, see page 63.

- When referring to a prefix, suffix or word-forming element, it is correct but not necessary to add a hyphen:

Consider the suffix '-ism'.

- Note the correct hyphenation of *wild-goose chase* (= 'hunt for wild geese') and *fine-tooth comb* (= 'comb with fine teeth'). *Fine toothcomb* is also considered correct by many (but not all) authorities. *Fine-toothed comb* must have the hyphen between *fine* and *toothed*.

Frequently lost hyphens

When two or more hyphenated words occur together in a sentence and have some part in common, the part they have in common may be omitted in all but the last instance.

15-year-olds and 16-year-olds > 15- and 16-year-olds
14th-century, 15th-century and 16th-century churches > 14th-, 15th- and 16th-century churches

In all such cases, the hyphen preceding the omitted part must be retained, as in the above examples.

   Errors in this regard are frequent and varied; for example:

✘ *14 and 15-year-olds*
✘ *14-15 year olds*
✘ *Those 20 and 30-somethings live alone.*
✘ *pre and post-war Britain*
✘ *The lenses are smudge and water-resistant.*
✘ *Made from weather and frost resistant material.*

The correct versions are:

✓ *14- and 15-year-olds*
✓ *14- to 15-year-olds*
✓ *Those 20- and 30-somethings live alone.*
✓ *pre- and post-war Britain*
✓ *The lenses are smudge- and water-resistant.*
✓ *Made from weather- and frost-resistant material.*

Note the difference between, for example, *her brother and sister-in-law* (= 'her brother and her sister-in-law') and *her brother- and sister-in-law* (= 'her brother-in-law and her sister-in-law').

Word-splitting hyphens

It is often necessary to split a word at the end of a line. If you are working on a word-processor, this will be done automatically; if you are writing by hand, you have to make your own decision about where to split.

There is often more than one place in which a word may be split correctly. As a general rule, try to split a word between any two of its basic structural elements:

broadminded > broad-minded or broadmind-ed
excitement > excite-ment or ex-citement
misunderstood > mis-understood or misunder-stood
collective > collect-ive or col-lective
expensive > expens-ive or ex-pensive
astronaut > astro-naut
prepare > pre-pare
occur > oc-cur

Where there is no obvious grammatical structure to the word, split at a suitable pronounceable point between syllables. If there is only one consonant, make the split before it:

thou-sand, trou-sers, etc

If there is more than one consonant, split between two consonants or after the first consonant of a group of three:

mur-der, get-ting, swim-ming, etc
spec-trum, dol-drums, etc

Never split a word in such a way that the part at the end of the line misleads the reader as to what is coming:

fastidious > ✓*fas-tidious* not ✗*fast-idious*
reinstall > ✓*re-install* not ✗*rein-stall*
therapist > ✓*ther-apist* not ✗*the-rapist*

The split should suggest the correct pronunciation of the word:

✓*spe-cial* not ✗*spec-ial*
✓*dep-recate* not ✗*de-precate*
✓*aristoc-racy* but ✓*aristo-cratic*
✓*bureauc-racy* but ✓*bureau-cratic*

Do not split words between letters that together represent a single sound, such as *th* = /th/, *ch* = /ch/, *sh* = /sh/, etc:

teacher > ✓*teach-er* not ✗*teac-her*

nor between letters if one of them is silent:

plumber > ✓*plumb-er* not ✗*plum-ber*

Do not split words of one syllable:

✓*wash-ing* but not ✗*wash-ed*

(Note also that some people consider it poor style to make a break in a word which leaves only the last two letters of the word on the second line. It is not entirely incorrect, but you may wish to avoid doing this to avoid offending those who do not like it.)

Split a hyphenated compound word at an already existing hyphen. Do not split the word at the end of a line in such a way as to require a further word-splitting hyphen:

✗*space-sav-ing*
✗*ill-con-ceived*

And finally, do not split personal names.

If you want more help with hyphenation, either choose a dictionary that shows how to hyphenate words or else buy a special hyphenation dictionary (of which there are several available in shops).

Summary of key points

- Two or more words that have to be understood as single elements in a sentence are generally hyphenated.
- Phrases formed with *well, better, best, ill, worse, worst, most* and *least* plus a past participle require a hyphen before a noun but (with the exception of *ill*) not elsewhere.
- Multi-word phrases acting as nouns are generally hyphenated, but hyphenation in two-word compound nouns is unpredictable.
- Phrasal verbs should not be hyphenated, but nouns and adjectives formed from phrasal verbs usually are.
- When two or more hyphenated words occur together in a sentence and have some part in common, the part they have in common may be omitted in all but the last compound but the hyphen preceding the omitted part must be retained in all the words.
- When splitting a word at the end of a line, make the split at a structurally or phonetically suitable place, and never where it could confuse the reader.

13
Apostrophes

There is not the faintest reason for persisting in the ugly and silly trick of peppering pages with these uncouth bacilli.

George Bernard Shaw

George Bernard Shaw was an advocate of spelling reform, and in his own writing he regularly omitted apostrophes. He would, for example, write *aint, dont, havnt, shant, shouldnt* and *wont* without apostrophes, using the apostrophe only where its omission (for example, *hell* for *he'll*) might suggest another word altogether.

English writers have not adopted Shaw's spelling recommendations, and like it or not, anyone who wants to spell correctly must get to grips with the rules governing the various uses of apostrophes.

The possessive apostrophe

One of the main uses of the apostrophe is to mark possessive forms:

John's books   *the boys' bikes*

The rule in its basic form is perfectly straightforward and comes in two parts.

First, the possessive form of a noun or name is made by adding *'s* to it:

the boy's dog (= 'the dog belonging to the boy')
the children's bikes (= 'the bikes belonging to the children')
James's wife (= 'the wife of James')
Robert Burns's poetry (= 'the poetry of Robert Burns')
my brothers-in-law's cars (= 'the cars belonging to my brothers-in-law')
the Laird of Cockpen's wig (= 'the wig belonging to the Laird of Cockpen')

But if the noun or name is plural and it already ends in *s*, add an apostrophe alone:

the boys' dog (= 'the dog belonging to the boys')
in two months' time (= 'after two months')

Exceptions: with singular names ending in *s*, usage is variable:

Moses' army or *Moses's army*

The simple rule here is: Write what you say. If you say /'mohziziz/, write *Moses's*, but if you say /'mohziz/, write *Moses'*. Similarly, depending on how you pronounce the words, you can correctly write *Burns's poetry* or *Burns' poetry* (but always *Burns Night* without an apostrophe).

Some compound nouns, originally possessive, are no longer written with an apostrophe:

Achilles' heel but *Achilles tendon*

Errors to watch for:

- ✗*Les' email*
  ✗*Gus' personal feelings*

The possessive forms should be *Les's* and *Gus's* because that is how the words would be said.

- ✗*childrens clothes*
  ✗*ladies shoe repair*

These need an apostrophe: *children's, ladies'*.

- ✗*childrens' clothes*
  ✗*mens' shoe repair*

The apostrophes are in the wrong place: *children's, men's*.

Note, however, that no apostrophe is needed in a compound noun written as a single word: ✓*menswear*.

Possessive pronouns do not have apostrophes:

hers, ours, yours, theirs, its, whose

Note in particular the difference between *its* (= 'of it') and *it's* (= 'it is' or 'it has'), and *whose* (= 'of whom') and *who's* (= 'who is' or 'who has').

In expressions with *sake*, there may or may not be an apostrophe:

for heaven's sake but *for goodness sake*

Plural nouns

The simple rule is that plural nouns *do not* need an apostrophe:

✗ *Easter holiday's*
✗ *pasta's and kebab's*
✗ *tomato's and lettuce's*
✗ *Property's for Sale or Rent*
✗ *CCTV camera's are in operation.*
✓ *Easter holidays*
✓ *pastas and kebabs*
✓ *tomatoes and lettuces*
✓ *Properties for Sale or Rent* (see page 121 for plurals of words ending in *y*)

Similarly with names:

I'm tired of keeping up with the Joneses, and the Smiths, and the Browns.
There were two Georges in my class in primary school.

Exceptions:

• The plurals of certain short words are often written with apostrophes:

  She gave me a list of do's and don'ts. (Note the position of the apostrophe in *don'ts.*)
  I feel there are really two me's at the moment.
  Are the puppies he's or she's?
  We have had several set-to's with them over this.

Forms without apostrophes are equally correct.

• Plurals of lower-case letters or of abbreviations written wholly or partly in lower-case letters take apostrophes for clarity:

All that remains to do is dot some i's and cross some t's.
There were some very close appeals for lbw's.
She's got two PhD's, or are they MPhil's?

Plurals of capital letters or of abbreviations, etc written in capital letters do not require apostrophes, except for clarity:

MPs   TVs   WCs
What we need is a couple of JCBs.
Write a row of I's (not . . . row of Is)

But if the abbreviations are written with full stops, apostrophes are again needed for clarity: *M.P.'s, Ph.D.'s, W.C.'s.*

The same is true for past tenses of abbreviations. An apostrophe may be needed for clarity:

The car needs to be M.O.T.'d or MOT'd.

If a plural word is being quoted in a sentence, it is often written with an apostrophe, though the apostrophe can be omitted:

There are too many if's, but's and possibly's in this proposal.

Similarly, if a plural noun is the title of a book, play, etc quoted in a sentence, it is better written with an apostrophe, though again it is correct to omit the apostrophe:

I've already seen three Macbeth's this year. (= three versions of *Macbeth*)

The plurals of single numbers are written with apostrophes:

Take away the 2's, then the 3's.

The plurals of longer numbers, dates, etc are better written without apostrophes, but it is not wrong to have one:

the 1970s or *the 1970's*

Omissions

Letters that have been omitted are usually indicated by apostrophes:

are not > aren't
cannot > can't
have not > haven't

he will > he'll
will not > won't
do not > don't (watch *do's and don'ts*)

Apostrophes are often used in this way in representations of informal speech:

She'd've done the same thing.
So'm I.
D'you like it?
I should never've trusted you!
That'd've made my day.
I know I shouldn't've said it.

When *and* is shortened to *n*, there should be *two* apostrophes:

cheese 'n' onion crisps
rock 'n' roll

Some shortened forms of words and phrases are written with apostrophes even though the non-contracted forms are no longer in use; for example:

o'clock (from *of the clock*)
ne'er-do-well (from *never-do-well*)
Hallowe'en (from *All Hallow Even*; *Halloween* is also correct)

Some contractions are out of date but still seen in poetry, etc:

e'en, o'er, 'tis or *'twas*

Many words that are in origin shortened forms are now fully accepted as words in their own right and are not written with apostrophes:

bra, bus, cello, decaff, exam, flu, gym, phone, plane, pram, etc

Apostrophes indicating the omission of letters may sometimes be found in place-names:

Bo'ness (in West Lothian = 'Borrowstounness')
Jo'burg (= Johannesburg).

Apostrophes may also be used to indicate the omission of numbers, e.g. in dates:

during the '70s and '80s (in this case, do not put an apostrophe
  before the *s*: ✘ *the '70's*)
That happened back in '97, I think.

Apostrophes in foreign languages

Certain languages, such as Arabic and Chinese, require apostrophes when transliterated into English:

the Noble Qur'an   *t'ai chi ch'uan*

Make sure you put the apostrophes in and get them in the right place. If in doubt, check in your dictionary.

(There are actually two ways of transliterating Chinese into English: one requires apostrophes and the other does not. Hence one sees both *ch'i* and *qi*, *t'ai chi ch'uan* and *tai ji quan* or *taijiquan*.)

Keyboarding apostrophes

Take care when keyboarding words or numbers with initial apostrophes. You may have to correct ones that face the wrong way:

not '*tis* but '*tis*
not *rock 'n' roll* but *rock 'n' roll*
not '*70s* but '*70s*

> ### *Summary of key points*
>
> - Possessives are formed by adding '*s* to a noun or name, unless the noun or name is plural and ends in *s*, in which case only an apostrophe is added.
> - Possessive forms of pronouns do not have apostrophes.
> - Plurals are not usually written with apostrophes.
> - Apostrophes are used to indicate where letters have been omitted.

14
Full stops in abbreviations

Abbreviations of words

Abbreviations that include the last letter of the short-ened word are written without full stops in British English:

Mr, Mrs, Dr, St, Ave, etc

Full stops are not incorrect, though, and are preferred in American English.

Abbreviations formed with numbers are never followed by full stops:

1st, 2nd, 3rd, 4th, 4to (= 'quarto')

Abbreviations not including the last letter of the word may be followed by a full stop:

adv., cent. (= 'century'), *doz., Jan., Sq., Tues., vol.,* etc

Nonetheless many of these abbreviations (especially

the months and the days of the week) are now usually written without full stops.

Abbreviations of names

Abbreviations of the names of countries, organizations, etc are usually written without full stops:

USA, UN, EU, etc

When the abbreviations are treated as words, they cannot be written with full stops:

Nato, UNESCO, UNICEF, etc

With people's initials it is equally correct to omit or write full stops, and in British English probably now commoner to omit them:

R B Burns or *R. B. Burns*

With abbreviations of names, add a full stop:

Robt. Burns, Geo. Davidson

Abbreviations of measurements

Abbreviations of metric measurements, of the temperature scales, and of compass directions, and the symbols for chemical elements are written without full stops:

cm, km, kg
10°C, 180°F
WSW, NNE
C, Fe, Pb, Z

Abbreviations of non-metric measurements may be written with or without full stops:

hr or *hr.*, *in* or *in.*

If the abbreviation includes the last letter of the word, there is usually no full stop:

ft, hr, mth, yr

If the abbreviation has a full stop in the singular, it will have one in the plural as well, and if not in the singular, then not in the plural:

hrs or *hrs.*

Abbreviations of degrees

Abbreviations of degrees and honours may be written with full stops, but are usually written without:

MA, BSc, PhD, MLitt, etc or *M.A., B.Sc., Ph.D., M.Litt.*, etc
OBE, KCVO, etc or *O.B.E.*, etc

Abbreviations of Latin words

Abbreviations of Latin words are usually written with full stops:

a.m., p.m., e.g., i.e., ibid., viz., etc

But there is an increasing tendency to write some of these (especially *am, pm, etc*) without full stops. If you are uncertain, follow your dictionary.

Other abbreviations

Other abbreviations written in capitals, are nowadays generally written without full stops (though in most cases full stops are not wrong):

AGM, CD, CV, MOT, PLC, VDU, etc

Two-letter abbreviations of single words

Abbreviations such as *TV* (= 'television') and *PS* (= 'postscript') should not be written with full stops.

Texting, Internet and email abbreviations

Abbreviations used in texting, on the Internet and in email are not written with full stops:

BFN (= 'bye for now')
HAND (= 'have a nice day')

15

Accents and diacritics

In many foreign languages, words are spelt not just with letters but also with accents and diacritics written above or below some of the letters; for example:

French *être, café, à, haïr, façade*
Spanish *fácil, mañana*
Italian *caffè*
German *Führer*

(In German, the ¨ is sometimes replaced by an *e*: *Fuehrer.*)

When a foreign word is used in English writing, it should always be spelt as it is in the original language. Take particular care with the accents and diacritics, that they are in the correct position and have the correct shape. If in any doubt, check in your dictionary and list the correct spellings in your spelling file. (In addition, note that it is normal practice to write a foreign word or words in italics if it is possible to do so.)

It is particularly important to write accents and diacritics correctly in foreign personal names and place-names; for example:

French *François, Françoise, Thérèse, Sèvres*
Spanish *José, Córdoba*
German *Jürgen, Würzburg*
Welsh *Siân*
Czech *Škoda, Dvořák*

However, if an established anglicized form of a place-name exists, use it, in which case no accents or diacritics are likely to be required:

Montreal not *Montréal*
Quebec not *Québec*
Pyrenees not *Pyrénées* (but *Pyrénées-Orientales* for the French department)
Rhone not *Rhône* (but *Côtes du Rhône* for the wine)
Catalonia not *Cataluña*
Munich not *München*

Many words of foreign origin are now so well established in English that they are treated as fully English words. There are two consequences of this: they are not written in italics, and they often lose their original accents and diacritics. For example, one can now write *cafe* or *café, cortege* or *cortège, crepe* or *crêpe, fete* or *fête, naive* or *naïve, role* or *rôle, suede* or (now only very rarely) *suède,* whereas words that are still considered foreign, such as *bête noire* and *tête-à-tête,* keep their accents at all times.

As can be seen from the above examples, usage is fluid, but the following rules of thumb can be applied:

- If the absence of an accent or diacritic would suggest an incorrect pronunciation of a word, do not drop it:

  façade not *facade*
  aperçu not *apercu*

- In words derived from French, keep the accent when the word ends in a single *e*:

  attaché, blasé, cliché, communiqué, consommé, exposé, fiancé, glacé, habitué, manqué, naïveté, passé, protégé, résumé, risqué, sauté, soufflé, but allow *cafe* (although *café* is preferable)

  If the word ends in a double *ee*, the accent is optional and often dropped:

  entree (or *entrée*), *fricassee, matinee, melee* (sometimes *mêlée*), *negligee, puree* (or *purée*), *soiree* (or *soirée*), *toupee*

  Note the two nouns which show a difference in spelling to match a difference in gender: masculine *fiancé, protégé,* feminine *fiancée; protégée.*

- Keep the accent in French *à la,* even when it is followed by a non-French word or name:

  à la mode
  chicken à la Colonel Sanders

16
Numbers and symbols

Numbers

Letters or figures?

Small numbers should be written as words:

After seven years in darkness, he was able to see again.
After six and a half hours Paul finally held up his hand as a signal to stop.

Larger numbers may be written in words, but numbers over ten, or over twelve, or from twenty upwards (authorities differ in their recommendations) are written in figures. Some authorities spell out numbers up to and including ninety-nine, which is perfectly correct though less common.

Apparently only 12 people had attempted the route Tom was suggesting, five of whom had died.
A simple 20-minute operation restored his sight.
We are working to prevent and cure blindness in over 30 countries.

Was every one of the remaining 59 days going to be equally hard?

Relatively complex large numbers are best written as figures:

There are exactly 2157 trees in this wood. I've counted them.

In mathematics and statements of measurements and amounts, figures are correct:

The sand dunes could be anything up to 7ft high.
The sledges weighed more than 80 kilograms.
It's over 100 kilometres to the Pole.
One survey found that some four-year-olds consume 8.5g of salt each day.
Help restore a person's sight by giving £17.

It is considered bad style by many authorities to begin a sentence with a number written in figures:

✗ *24 hours after his surgery, he had his bandages removed.*
✓ *Twenty-four hours after his surgery, he had his bandages removed.*

An exception to this is when the number is followed by further words to which it is linked by hyphens, when figures are generally preferred:

Twenty-six-year-old Mary Smith had an unexpected visitor on Saturday night.
26-year-old Mary Smith had an unexpected visitor on Saturday night.

Fractions
Fractions should be written out in full:

✓ *More than three-quarters of the women in this region are illiterate.*
✗ *More than ¾ of the women in this region are illiterate.*

Commas in numbers and dates

There is no need to insert a comma in a four-figure number, though it is not wrong to do so:

2157 trees or *2,157 trees*

In larger numbers, commas are required:

14,507
2,504,678

Exception: do not put a comma in a number in an address:

Her address is 1075 Yonge Street.

Commas are not required in dates, but are still acceptable:

✓ *She was born on 4 February 1938.*
✓ *She was born on 4 February, 1938.*

Symbols

&

This symbol, called an ampersand, should in general only be used in the names of businesses, and then only if the businesses themselves use it:

Marks & Spencer

It should not be used as a replacement for 'and' in normal writing, but to save space and expense it may be used in advertisements:

Floor-laying & Sanding Specialists, Domestic & Commercial
All Types of Metal & Wood Fencing Supplied & Erected

Asterisk

Asterisks are often used to avoid spelling out swear-words:

F**k it! The computer's crashed again!

A dash may also be used for this purpose:

The f—ing computer's crashed again!

@

The 'at' sign is probably most used in email addresses nowadays:

j.smith@adnot.co.uk

It may also be used in statements of prices:

six lamps @ £14.99

#

The 'hash' mark is used in American English, but not yet commonly in British English, to mean 'number':

America's #1 record company

%

In general writing, spell out 'per cent' in words:

The population of Poland is 90 per cent Roman Catholic.

Use the % symbol only in more technical writing.

Slash

A slash is used to present alternatives:

members and/or guests
He/she may earn up to £200 a day.

A slash may mean 'per' along with other abbreviations:

£20/hr

And a slash may be used to link separate years indicating a period of time:

the 2004/2005 school year

17
Names

Names do not always obey the general rules of English spelling. For example, *Sheila, Keith, Madeira,* etc do not follow the '*i* before *e*' rule (see page 107).

Only a few examples of hard-to-spell or frequently misspelt names are given here. If you come across others you find hard to remember, note them in your spelling book.

Aaron	*Botticelli*
Abu Dhabi	*Boulogne*
Aegean	*Brahms*
Afghanistan	*Britain, British, Briton*
Algeria, Algiers	*Britannia*
Anthony	*Brittany* (in France)
Arctic, Antarctic	*Bruegel* or *Brueghel*
Bacchus	*Buddha, Buddhism*
Bahrain	*Caernarvon, Caernarfon*
Beethoven	*Caerphilly*
Bhutan	*Caesar*
Bordeaux	*Canaan*

Caribbean

Carlisle (town), Carlyle
  (family name)

Cheyenne

Christmas

Cincinnati

Colombia (South America),
  Columbia (USA)

Connecticut

Czech

Delhi

Djibouti

Dodecanese

February

Gandhi

Gauguin

Geoffrey

Ghana

Gloucester

Guatemala

Guernsey

Guyana

Hawaii

Haydn

Hungary

Iroquois

Jacqueline

January

Jonathan

Leicester

Leonard

Liechtenstein

Liszt

Llandudno

Llanelli

Llewelyn

Luxembourg

Machiavelli, Machiavellian

Madagascar

Madeira

Marseilles (also often spelt
  Marseille, as in French),
  Marseillaise

Massachusetts

Mediterranean

Mendelssohn

Michael

Michelangelo

Middlesbrough

Mississippi

Morocco

Mozambique

Muhammad, Mohammed

Neanderthal

Nebuchadnezzar

Nicaragua

Nicholas

Oedipus

Peloponnese

Pennsylvania

Philadelphia

Philippines

Pharaoh

Picasso

Piccadilly
Pittsburgh
Portuguese
Pyrenees
Qatar
Qur'an
Rebecca
Rembrandt
Saturday
Seychelles
Shakespeare

Sioux
Strasbourg
Tchaikovsky
Thailand
Tuesday
Uruguay
Venezuela
Wednesday
Worcester
Zaïre
Zimbabwe

18
British and American English

We have really everything in common with America nowadays, except, of course, language.

Oscar Wilde

There are many differences between British and American spelling, both in general spelling rules and in individual words. The main differences are outlined in this chapter.

ae or *e*

In words that can be spelt both *ae* and *e*, British English generally has the *ae* spelling, while in American English *e* is standard:

British English *anaemia, anaesthetic, haemoglobin,* etc
American English *anemia, anesthetic, hemoglobin,* etc

In some other words, American English accepts both *ae* and *e* spellings:

aesthetics or *esthetics*
archeology or *archaeology*
encyclopedia or *encyclopaedia*

Words that begin with *aer-* in British English also begin with *aer-* in American English (*aerobics, aerosol*) but note British English *aeroplane*, American English *airplane*.

ce, se

Some words that end in *ce* in British English are spelt *se* in American English:

British English *defence, offence, pretence*
American English *defense, offense, pretense*
British English *licence* (noun), *license* (verb); *practice* (noun), *practise* (verb)
American English *license* (noun and verb), *practice* (noun and verb)

Hyphens

American English uses fewer hyphens than British English. To take just one example, in American English words formed with *non-* (= 'not') are generally written as single words (*nonmember, nonsmoker*) whereas in British English they are normally hyphenated (*non-member, non-smoker*).

-ise, -ize

In verbs that in British English can end in either *-ise* or *-ize* (e.g. *equalise* or *equalize*), in American English the ending is always spelt *-ize*.

When the ending is spelt with a *y*, it is always spelt *-yse* in British English and *-yze* in American English:

British English *analyse, paralyse*
American English *analyze, paralyze*

Single and double *l*

Where British English doubles a final *l* before a word-ending such as *-ed* or *-ing* (see page 153), in American English the final *l* is *not* doubled:

British English *equalled, travelling, traveller, counsellor*
American English *equaled, traveling, traveler, counselor*

Note also British English *chilli, jeweller, jewellery, marvellous, woollen* but American English *chili* or *chilli, jeweler, jewelry, marvelous, woolen*.

On the other hand, in some words where British English has a single *l*, American English has *ll*:

British English *appal, distil, enrol, enthral, fulfil, instil* or *instill, skilful, wilful*
American English *appall, distill, enroll, enthrall, fulfill, instill, skillful, willful* or less commonly *wilful*

-logue, -log

British English *catalogue* and *dialogue*, American English *catalog* or *catalogue*, *dialog* or *dialogue* (the *-log* forms being the preferred variants). But in both British and American English, *analog* is the form used in computing: *an analog computer*.

oe or e

oe in British English; usually *e* in American English:

British English *amoeba, diarrhoea, foetus*
American English *amoeba* (*ameba* in technical language), *diarrhea, fetus*

-our, -or

Most words that end in *-our* in British English end in *-or* in American English:

British English *behaviour, colour, favour, flavour, harbour, honour,* etc
American English *behavior, color, favor, flavor, harbor, honor,* etc

In American English, *glamour* is the preferred spelling, but *glamor* is also correct.

Single and double *p*

In British English, the final *p* of *kidnap* and *worship* is doubled before a word-ending such as *-ing*, *-ed* and *-er*:

kidnapping, kidnapped, kidnappers; worshipping, worshipped, worshipper

In American English, spellings with one *p* or two *p*'s are equally correct.

re, er

Most words that end in *-re* in British English end in *-er* in American English:

British English *centre, fibre, litre, meagre, metre, sombre, spectre, theatre*, etc
American English *center, fiber, liter, meager, meter, somber, specter, theater*, etc

Not all words in American English obey this rule: *acre, macabre, massacre, mediocre* and *ogre*.

Vocabulary items spelt differently in British and American English

British English	American English
axe	*ax*
carburettor	*carburetor*
cheque	*check*
chequered	*checkered*

British English	American English
cigarette	*cigarette* (also *cigaret*)
cosy	*cozy*
disc (see also page 77)	*disk*
doughnut	*doughnut* or *donut*
draught and *draft*	*draft*
grey	*gray*
jail and *gaol*	*jail*
kerb	*curb*
liquorice	*licorice*
manoeuvre	*maneuver*
mollusc	*mollusk*
mould	*mold*
moult	*molt*
moustache	*mustache* or *moustache*
omelette	*omelette* or *omelet*
pedlar (but *drug peddler*)	*peddler*
phoney	*phony*
plough	*plow*
prise (= 'force with a lever')	*prize*
programme, program (see page 87)	*program*
pyjamas	*pajamas*
sceptic	*skeptic*
smoulder	*smolder*
storey	*story*
sulphur	*sulfur*
tyre	*tire*
vice (tool)	*vise*

Appendix: Technical terms used in this book

accent
1. A person's accent is the way in which he or she pronounces words.
2. An accent is a small mark written above a vowel either to indicate a particular pronunciation, as in *raison d'être* or *résumé*, or to show the position of the main stress in a word, as in the Spanish name *José*.
3. Accent is another word for *stress*.

adjective
An adjective is a describing word, such as *big, angry, poor, red,* etc.

adverb
An adverb is a word that describes how or where or when, etc: *quickly, badly, suddenly, very, quite, slightly, here, there, now, then, today,* etc.

affix
An affix is a *prefix* or a *suffix.*

assimilation
Assimilation is a process in speech by which one sound in a word changes to become the same as or more like an adjacent sound. Assimilation has, for example, given rise to sets of similar prefixes in English: *con-* (as in *convict*) has become *com-* before *b* in *combine* and before *m* in *communicate*, and *col-* before *l* in *colleague*; and *in-* (as in *inevitable*) has become *im-* before *p* in *impossible*, *il-* before *l* in *illegal*, and *ir-* before *r* in *irregular.*

combining form
A combining form is a word-forming element such as *electro-*, *geo-*, *hydro-*, *-graphy*, *-logy*, *-lysis* or *-metry* that can combine to form words: *geography, geometry, geology, hydrology, hydrolysis, electrolysis,* etc. Combining forms can also be added to existing words: *electromagnetic, geophysics, hydroelectricity.* Combining forms are generally of Latin or Greek origin.

compound
A compound word is one that is constructed from two or more smaller words: *teacup, pigsty, textbook, sky-blue, mind-blowing, heartbroken,* etc.

consonant
See *vowel*.

derivative
A derivative is a word that is formed by adding a prefix or more often a suffix to another word. For example, *leader* is a derivative of *lead*, *existence* is a derivative of *exist*, *replay* is a derivative of *play*.

diacritic
A diacritic is a small mark written above or below a letter to indicate that it is to be pronounced in a particular way. Diacritics include *accents*, the cedilla (as in *façade*) and the tilde (as in *mañana*).

digraph
A digraph is a sequence of two letters that together represent a single sound, such as *th* and *ng* in *thing*, or *ch* and *ea* in *cheat*.

diminutive
A diminutive is a word that denotes something of a small size, e.g. *birdie*.

diphthong
A diphthong consists of two vowel sounds spoken as if they were a single sound, e.g. /ay/, /ow/, /oy/.

direct speech
Direct speech is the actual words spoken by someone: *'I'll come tomorrow,'* he promised. Indirect speech is the description of what someone said rather than their actual words: *He promised he would come the next day*.

entry
An entry in a dictionary is the section of the text providing information about a word.

etymology
The etymology of a word is its origin and history.

hard c/g
Hard *c* and hard *g* are the sounds /k/ and /g/ respectively, as in *can* and *get*. Soft *c* and *g* are the sounds /s/ and /j/, as in *cent* and *gem*.

headword
A headword is the word (or words) defined or explained in an entry in a dictionary or other reference book.

homograph
Homographs are words that are spelt the same but pronounced differently, e.g. the metal *lead* and a dog's *lead*.

homonym
Homonyms are words that are identical in both sound and spelling: the *light* of the moon and a *light* meal.

homophone
Homophones are words that are pronounced the same but spelt differently, e.g. *beach* and *beech*.

indirect speech
See *direct speech*.

inflection
Inflection is the process of adding a suffix to a word or changing the form of a word to indicate plurals, different tenses, etc: *book > books, man > men, walk > walked, swim > swam*.

The words *books, men, walked, swam* can also be said to be inflections of *book, man, walk, swim*.

mnemonic
A mnemonic is a word, phrase, rhyme or anything else that helps you to learn or remember something, such as the rhyme that goes '30 days hath September, April, June and November . . .' which helps you to remember how many days there are in each of the months of the year.

noun
A noun is a word used as the name of a person, animal, place, thing, feeling, process, etc, e.g. *box, cat, John, France, fear, justice, refinement*, etc.

object
The object of a verb is whoever or whatever is receiving the action of the verb, such as 'a biscuit' in *Martha ate a biscuit*.

participle
Present participles are the forms of verbs that end in *-ing*: *coming, going, running*, etc.

Past participles often end in *-ed* (*marched, talked*, etc), but may have other forms (*eaten, spoken, written, bought, held, swam*, etc).

phrasal verb
Phrasal verbs are combinations of simple verbs such as *get, give, put, send* or *take* with adverbs such as *in, out* or *off* or prepositions such as *for* or *with*, or both: *get back, give off, hanker after, knock down, pick off, put up with*.

prefix
A prefix is a word-forming element that is added to the beginning of a word to form a new word (e.g. *un-* in *unknown*, *re-* in *replay*).

preposition
A preposition is a word that shows the relationship of one noun to another, e.g. *for, in, of, on, with*.

schwa
Schwa is the name given to the weak vowel heard in *ago* and *father*.

silent letter
A silent letter is one that is written but not pronounced, such as the *k* of *know* and *knee* or the *b* of *crumb* and *lamb*.

soft c/g
See *hard c/g*.

stem
A stem is a word to which an affix has been added to form a new word. For example, *warm* is the stem of *warmth*, *swim* is the stem of *swimming*. *Fool* is the stem of *foolish*, *foolish* is the stem of *foolishly* and *foolishness*.

stress
A vowel or a syllable is said to be stressed when it is pronounced with greater force or loudness than the other vowels or syllables in the word. For example, the stress is

on the first syllable of *photograph*, the second syllable of *photography* and the third syllable of *photographic*.

subject

The subject of a verb is the person or thing performing the action of the verb, e.g. *Martha ate a biscuit.*

suffix

A suffix is a word-forming element that is added to the end of a word to form a new word or to indicate plurals, tenses, etc; e.g. *-ness* in *goodness*, *-ing* in *writing*, *-er* in *teacher*.

syllable

A syllable is a section of speech consisting of one vowel sound together with the consonants that precede or follow it. For example, the words *a, and, but, think* and *stretch* are all single syllables. *Spelling, occur, limit, market* and *number* have two syllables. *Surprising, consonant, history* and *indicate* have three syllables, *dictionary* and *equivalent* have four syllables, *probability* has five syllables, and *invisibility* has six. If you say any word very slowly, you will automatically split it up into syllables.

Sometimes a syllable may be formed by a consonant sound, such as /l/. For example, *table* and *Bible* have two syllables and *possible* and *probable* have three.

verb

A verb is a word that describes an action, process or state, e.g. *be, become, bring, come, feel, sing,* etc.

vowel

1. As *sounds*, vowels and consonants differ in the way they are produced in speech. For example, if you say the word *a*, you will notice that the air flows freely out of your mouth without restriction, whereas if you say *cat* or *bat*, the flow of air is briefly cut off when you pronounce the sounds

written as *c*, *b*, and *t*; and if you say *fat* or *sat*, the flow of air is slightly restricted when you pronounce the sounds written as *f* and *s*, although it is not completely cut off.

A sound that is produced without any restriction of the flow of air through the mouth and throat is a *vowel*, and a sound that is produced with partial or complete restriction of the flow of air is a *consonant*.

2. As far as the *alphabet* is concerned, vowels are those letters which normally represent vowel sounds and consonants are those letters which generally represent consonant sounds. So *a*, *e*, *i*, *o* and *u* are vowels, and *b*, *c*, *d*, *f*, *g*, *h*, *j*, *k*, *l*, *m*, *n*, *p*, *q*, *r*, *s*, *t*, *v*, *w*, *x* and *z* are consonants. *Y* is normally included with the consonants, but actually serves as both consonant and vowel: it is, for example, a consonant in *yes*, *year* and *you*, but a vowel in words like *my* and *silly*.

3. Vowel sounds vary in length, and can be divided into short vowels and long vowels. The short vowels are /a/, /e/, /i/, /o/, /oo/, /u/ and /ə/; all the others are long vowels.

word-ending
A word-ending is a *suffix*.

word-forming element
Prefixes, *suffixes* and *combining forms* are word-forming elements. Other word-forming elements derive from, for example, Latin, e.g. *sist*, *cid*, *fid*, etc (see page 185).

Bibliography

R E Allen, *One Step Ahead: Spelling* (Oxford University Press: Oxford 2002)

E Carney, *A Survey of English Spelling* (Routledge: London and New York 1994)

—— *English Spelling* (Routledge: London and New York 1997)

G Davidson, *Chambers Guide to Grammar and Usage* (Chambers: Edinburgh 1996)

T McArthur (ed.), *The Oxford Companion to the English Language* (Oxford University Press: Oxford 1992)

A Seaton, *Understanding Spelling* (Learners Publishing: Singapore 2001)

L Todd, *The Cassell Guide to Punctuation* (Cassell: London 1995)

R L Trask, *The Penguin Guide to Punctuation* (Penguin Books: Harmondsworth 1997)

Index of difficult words

This book is full of 'difficult words'. It is not, however, the purpose of this index to list them all individually.

If you need to check up on the spelling of a particular word, the best place to look is in your dictionary. Words with unpredictable endings are not a problem, because if you can spell the beginning of the word correctly, you will find the word in your dictionary even if you aren't quite sure about how to spell the end of it. However, if you are not sure of the correct spelling of the *beginning* of a word, it may be difficult to find the word in a dictionary at all: you may well be looking in completely the wrong place. You will not, for example, find *acumulate* on a page near *acute*, because the correct spelling is *accumulate* with two *c*'s.

The purpose of this index, therefore, is not to point the way to *all* the 'difficult words' in this book but rather to words with 'difficult beginnings'. Not only are the correct spellings given, but also common misspellings (marked with ✘) and, where helpful, cross-references to the page(s) where more information on the correct spelling can be found. Included among the misspellings are some phonetic spellings, such as *eejis*, that no-one is actually likely to think of writing but which might help you find the word you are looking for (*aegis*).

Remember that there are also lists of frequently misspelt or confused words in Chapters 3, 4 and 5. Remember also that if you can't find the word you are looking for, you should look in Chapters 6 and 7 under the *sound* that is causing you difficulty. See the Index of Sounds on page 318. Alternatively, if your problem lies with a particular *category* of word, check in the Index of Topics on page 319, which will direct you to the appropriate section of the book.

Index of sounds

See pages ix to xi for an explanation of the symbols used.

Index of topics